MW01702502

# 30 Days of JOY

*for busy married couples*

**Chris and Jennifer Coursey**


Version 1.2

Published by
**Shepherd's House Inc.**
P.O. Box 2376
East Peoria, Illinois 61611

www.joystartshere.com

A LIFE MODEL™ BOOK

# Thirty Days of JOY
*for busy married couples*

By: Chris and Jen Coursey



ISBN 978-1-935629-15-3

Printed by:
Shepherd's House Inc.
PO Box 2376
East Peoria, IL 61611
www.joystartshere.com
Order from www.lifemodel.org



Cover design by Kurt Smith.
Pictures by *Ross & Amy Mulder Photography*, amymulderphotography.com.

Thanks to Jen Hopp for editing this book.

Information contained in this marriage handbook is used with permission from Pastor Ed Khouri and Dr. Jim Wilder from *Connexus for a thriving community* at www.joystartshere.com.

Immanuel Process and relational circuit information is based on the work of Dr. Karl and Charlotte Lehman at www.kclehman.com, www.immanuelapproach.com and www.outsmartingyourself.org.

# Table of Contents

# Thirty Day Checklist

- ☐ Day 1 Exercise - *Relational Circuit Checklist*
- ☐ Day 2 Exercise - *Joy Smiles With Music*
- ☐ Day 3 Exercise - *Appreciation Exercise*
- ☐ Day 4 Exercise - *Feeding, Fun And Food*
- ☐ Day 5 Exercise - *Overwhelm - When To Disengage*
- ☐ Day 6 Exercise - *Getting Prefrontal*
- ☐ Day 7 Exercise - *Relational Circuits And Cravings*
- ☐ Day 8 Exercise - *Joy Smiles Without Music*
- ☐ Day 9 Exercise - *Immanuel Practice*
- ☐ Day 10 Exercise - *Love On Your Spouse*
- ☐ Day 11 Exercise - *Joy Stories*
- ☐ Day 12 Exercise - *Cravings, Food And Bonding*
- ☐ Day 13 Exercise - *Maturity Inventory*
- ☐ Day 14 Exercise - *Massage*
- ☐ Day 15 Exercise - *Strength And Weakness*
- ☐ Day 16 Exercise - *Bonding With Fun And Play*
- ☐ Day 17 Exercise - *Immanuel Intervention For Irritations*
- ☐ Day 18 Exercise - *Show And Share Your Joy*
- ☐ Day 19 Exercise - *Food, Bonding And Blessing*
- ☐ Day 20 Exercise - *Intro To Skill Eleven: Return To Joy*
- ☐ Day 21 Exercise - *Three, Three And Three Appreciation*
- ☐ Day 22 Exercise - *Sandwich Making*
- ☐ Day 23 Exercise - *Tender Responses: Missing In Action*
- ☐ Day 24 Exercise - *Appreciation Card*
- ☐ Day 25 Exercise - *Pray Like Jesus Prays*
- ☐ Day 26 Exercise - *Generational Strengths And Weaknesses*
- ☐ Day 27 Exercise - *Love That Serves*
- ☐ Day 28 Exercise - *Food And Joy*
- ☐ Day 29 Exercise - *Sexuality Exercise*
- ☐ Day 30 Exercise - *Looking Back but Moving Forward*

## *Your marriage is worth it.*

If you are like us and most married couples we know, you have a lot on your plate. Your days are full. Activities, work, schedules, to-do lists, chores and, in our case, children fill up the daily planner. For us, we are talking about young, energetic, active children who require time, joyful attention and much, much love. By the end of the day exhaustion sets in. No, wait a minute. Exhaustion sets in when the alarm clock goes off first thing in the morning! There are so many demands that your days fly by in a flurry of busyness. Somewhere in the middle of it all, many couples feel their marriage has lost its flavor. This wasn't planned, but joy levels are not what you want or dreamed they would be. Over time your marriage starts to feel like the blues song B.B. King made famous, "The Thrill Is Gone." Yes, something is missing. We would say it's time for joy. Your marriage is worth a joy makeover.

## *Joy is God's gift to you.*

There is hope. Whether your marriage suffers from busyness or boredom, joy is the gift God wants to share with you. Joy also happens to be an excellent solution to marital deprivations, distress and distractions. Relational joy is what you were designed for. When joy levels sink life starts to feel painful and overwhelming. Joy is the reason we created this skill guide. All you have to do is carve out 15-20 minutes each day for thirty days. Yes, this is a big commitment in your already busy schedule. We think your marriage is worth it. We believe you think your marriage is worth it too, otherwise you would not holding this book in your hands. Turn off the television. Put down your phone. Protect your time. Give joy a time slot in your daily routine. Whether you practice your daily exercise in the morning, over lunch, after dinner or before bed, you will be pleasantly surprised and refreshed. Joy does that, you know!

We have personally gone through every exercise. We strategically crafted the exercises to invigorate your marriage. Much like us, you will be delighted to discover that your energy levels increase as you feel seen, cherished and valued doing the exercises together. You may, no, you *will* lack motivation at times to do the exercises but give them a try. The results will speak for themselves.

## *Joy changed us. Joy can change you.*

The reason we put this introductory "joy taster" resource together is, simply, because joy changed us! Joy has radically transformed our marriage. Joy is easy to start but hard to sustain over time. All of us can benefit from a short book like this to guide and motivate us along with daily exercises, encouragement and tips.

Thanks to the training, influence and resources from Life Model Works; Dr. Jim and Kitty Wilder; Pastor Ed and Maritza Khouri; Dr. Karl and Charlotte Lehman, we have created a fresh, dynamic series of exercises based on THRIVE Training and *Joy Rekindled* Marriage Retreats so that busy couples can practice the nineteen brain skills (*see Appendix B.*) We actively use the Immanuel Lifestyle as a way of relating and interacting with each other as well as our children. You will see a generous sprinkling of these components and more throughout this handbook. The exercises contain bonus questions, personal thoughts, additional information and Life Model Works resources for you to pursue for more detail and depth.

We respect that you are busy - very very busy. While your plates are full we want your relational joy cups to overflow. While there is a lot of good information in this handbook the goal is to *practice joy with your mate*. You will get out of the exercises what you put into them. Because we have personally gone through each exercise we can honestly say that our joy levels have increased. We pray your joy levels increase and may God richly bless you and your marriage as you begin this journey of joy.

"Be joyful always; pray continually; give thanks in all circumstances, for this is God's will for you in Christ Jesus" 1 Thessalonians 5:16-18 (NIV).

Chris and Jen Coursey

# When I Feel Upset

Building joy is life-giving. You and your spouse require "glad to be together" joy moments in order to relationally thrive. Because we live in a fallen world where things can go wrong and often do, many of us have suffered from low-joy moments that proved painful at some point in life. You may have felt overwhelmed, rejected, betrayed, neglected or abandoned, which can leave scars. The bad news is this: *relationships are a source of our distress*. The good news is this: *God uses relationships with Himself and His people as an instrument to heal hurts and wounds*. Joy gives us the strength to manage what we feel and recover.

As you work your way through the *Thirty Days of JOY* handbook, some of the exercises may bring up pain because, simply, building joy can be painful. Sounds ironic, doesn't it? This does not mean we should stop building joy; rather, we use these moments as opportunities for God to rebuild a new place in our identity and character. We do not want you to be surprised if this happens, but we do want you to be prepared with a few helpful tips.

- **Rely on quiet as your friend.** When strong feelings emerge one of the best responses is to catch your breath, calm down and quiet yourself.
- **Respect your limits.** Stretching is good but forcing or trying to be strong will backfire. Joy should always lead to rest so we want a healthy combination of joy and rest for our interactions.
- **Recharge with appreciation** Remembering joy brings us joy in a package we call appreciation. When you feel off-line, non-relational, tired and burned out, take at least 3 minutes of active appreciation and focus on what brings you joy. This simple step can start a dead battery on a wintry day!
- **Reach out to Immanuel.** You will learn simple steps in this handbook that introduce how to rely on Immanuel to bring healing and comfort to the war-torn places that need a bit of encouragement and healing. Some of us are high energy people who need to exercise, walk or run to feel connected to God while others pursue quiet and low-energy activities. Do what works for you.
- **Request prayer from a support team.** Prayer works. Turn to those

you trust and ask them to pray for you and your spouse when things become painful or difficult.

- **Read about the brain's Verbal Logical Explainer** (VLE) explained by Dr. Karl and Charlotte Lehman. Quite simply, the VLE is a term used to describe the brain's requirement to find explanations that interpret and justify our upset. What tends to happen for couples is a deadly dynamic where we blame and accuse each other because we are hurting or upset when, in reality, some of our upset may be anchored in the past. Our intense reactions may have very little to do with what or who is actually in front of us! This is a must-read for couples and we encourage you to explore Dr. Lehman's websites, www.outsmartingyourself.org for more on this fascinating topic.
- **Remind each other to rest and care for the needs that arise** as you go through your practice time. It helps to have permission from each other to rest, step out for a breath of fresh air when interactions heat up or do what is necessary in order to return to relational mode. Both of you want to practice validation and comfort when problems arise. Validation says, "My, you are really hurting by what I said aren't you? I am very sorry for hurting you like this." Comfort says, "I am so sorry I did this to you. How can I rebuild your trust and make you feel safe once again?"
- **Return to relational mode as soon as possible.** If we fall into a frozen lake the last thing we want to do is hang out and practice the breast stroke. We want to return to shore and warmth ASAP before we freeze! The same is true during moments we fall out of relational mode. Practice your relational circuit exercises so that you return to relational mode and avoid casualties with your words and actions. Your relational circuits provide the resources to navigate relational conflicts and recover from moments that are painful.
- **Remember what is important.** As you begin to calm down from your upset, you will do well and your nervous system will thank you if you start to remember joy and the special times with your spouse. This step helps you see each other through heaven's eyes, as God sees him or her. You can ask, "God, what do You want me to know about my spouse? What do You see here?"

These are a few simple suggestions to help you better navigate interactions as you build joy. We suggest you take your time going through the exercises. Take care of yourselves and have a ton of fun!

# Day One

We start this thirty-day training by warming up your relational circuits for one simple reason: *how much you gain from this skill guide largely depends on the status of your relational circuits.* We cannot stress this enough. If your relational circuits are off or dimmed, you will experience very little joy doing the exercises. If you are in relational mode, you will notice that you are getting much more out of the time. Heck, you may even smile!

Relational circuit awareness (also called RC's) has made a noticeable difference in our marriage and family. When we are in relational mode everything seems to go better. Joy grows. Interactions are satisfying. When dimmed, well, let's just say we notice life and interactions are much more difficult. You will notice a common thread where we frequently refer to relational circuits to better help you develop the awareness of whether your RC's are on or dimmed. We want you to discover, first-hand, the rewards of having your RC's on as well as the cost of having them dimmed. This RC exercise is your first step in the journey of joy.

# Relational Circuit Checklist

1. Use the RC checklist on page 6 to determine if your relational circuits are warmed up and on.
2. If you feel non-relational, practice getting your relational circuits on by using one of the *Shalom My Body* exercises or by remembering appreciation. (*Refer to the Relational Circuit Checklist for details or visit the* ***Chris Coursey - THRIVE*** *channel on YouTube for a demonstration by Dr. Jim Wilder.*)
3. Discuss with your spouse:
    a. What does it feel like when your relational circuits are warmed and on?
    b. How does it feel when your relational circuits are dimmed or off? Compare the two.
    c. Are there patterns or circumstances when you notice your relational circuits usually go off?
4. Share with your spouse what you notice and appreciate when you observe moments he or she is in relational mode.
    a. Example: "When you are in relational mode I really enjoy watching you play with the children and seeing how your face lights up as you have fun."

**Bonus 1:**

- Express aspects of your spouse's character that you admire while you hold hands and maintain eye contact.

**Bonus 2:**

- Discuss how your spouse's responses help or hurt the status of your relational circuits. What do you each need when your RC's are down? A wise man once said, "Two are better than one, because they have a good reward for their labor. For if they fall, one will lift up his companion. But woe to him who is alone when he falls, for he has no one to help him up" Ecclesiastes 4:9-10, (NKJV). As a married couple, we are in the best possible position to help our spouse when he or she falls out of relational mode. We hope this exercise gives you a jumpstart toward staying joyful and proactive in your relationship.

**Bonus 3:**

- Measure your joy levels so you can then compare the results of your joy growth when you finish the exercises in this book. Visit www.joyq.joystartshere.com to register and take your free assessment.

## Additional Information:

Here is an abbreviated list to help you identify what relational circuits feel like:

**RC's On:**

I feel warm and open; I notice less tension in my muscles. I feel peaceful and caring. I am more connected within myself and with my spouse. I am grounded, clear, warm, engaged, peaceful, caring, flexible and relaxed.

**RC's Off:**

I feel tense, "dark", snappy, negative, mad, irritable and I don't care about my spouse or what she/he feels and thinks. I feel rigid, anxious, angry, tired, "blah," impatient, brooding, restless, cravings, non-relational, sharp (abrupt), critical, judgmental, snappy and annoyed.

**Note:** The *Shalom My Body* exercises mentioned in Step 2 refer to simple exercises you can practice to quiet fear and anger responses in your body. As you quiet and calm these nervous system responses you feel more peaceful and more present. Your relational circuits are more likely to come on after these exercises. If you are still confused about relational circuits read page 64.

## Chris and Jen Thoughts:

*We were driving in the car while on vacation after a short night of sleep. Our boys went to bed late and were up way too early. Everyone was feeling "crispy" and tired. We decided to try this exercise and noticed an immediate difference in terms of looking at the status of our relational circuits while also finding descriptions of how we feel in each state. What was most remarkable was how we realized patterns in each other and our relationship when one of us is in the "dimmed" mode while the other is more relational. We tend to relate with each other much like a teeter totter with one in relational mode and the other not in relational mode and when one of us encounters our partner in non-relational mode it quickly triggers the shut off switch and soon we both have fallen out of relational mode.*

*This was a meaningful exercise for us and we hope it is for you too!*

## Additional Resources:

- *Belonging* module in the Connexus for a thriving community at www.joystartshere.com
- *Jesus In Mind Talks*, Volumes 10, 12 and 19 at www.joystartshere.com
- *Outsmarting Yourself* by Dr. Karl and Charlotte Lehman
    - www.kclehman.com, www.outsmartingyourself.org, www.immanuelapproach.com
- *THRIVE 52-week Skill Guides* at www.thrivetoday.org
- *THRIVE-at-Home* Online Curriculum at www.thrivetoday.org

## *DAY 1 NOTES - THOUGHTS - OBSERVATIONS:*

# Relational Circuit Checklist

**Relational Circuits Checklist Short Form**
Adapted from the new Connexus for a thriving community designed by Pastor Ed Khouri and Dr. Jim Wilder www.joystartshere.com, based on the work of Karl Lehman M.D. www.kclehman.com.

1. I just want to make a problem, person or feeling go away.
2. I don't want to listen to what others feel or say.
3. My mind is "locked onto" something upsetting.
4. I don't want to be connected to __? (Someone I usually like)
5. I just want to get away or fight, or I freeze.
6. I more aggressively interrogate, judge and fix others.

If I answered YES to any of these, my relational circuits are OFF. Everything related to relational conflict and my skill guide training will turn out better when my relational circuits are back ON.

**Restoration Steps when Relational Circuits are OFF:**
**My goal** is to perceive the Lord's presence, tell Jesus about my pain, and receive His comfort so that I can get my relational connection circuits back on line.

**My strategy** is to quiet my body and then talk to God about my emotions and thoughts, even if I don't perceive His presence yet. I invite the Lord to be with me and help me perceive His presence. I tell others how God's peace helped me.

**My steps:**

1. **God's peace and rest for my body.** Physically reduce my fear and adrenaline, activate my stress reduction system (Parasympathetic response in Step 3), and physically enter a quiet state for my body and mind.

2. **Shalom my soul.** I talk to God directly about my emotions and thoughts, even though I do not perceive His presence. I do NOT talk to God about the other person I am upset with as that keeps my relational circuits OFF!
3. **Lament with God.** I feel sad about those things that grieve both God and me. This activates the ventromedial circuits and parasympathetic system in my brain. (This means I have an easier time moving from my anger state.) For example, I can write down all the things about my current situation that could make me sad and what makes God sad for me. I tell God these things with authentic expression.
4. **Grow my appreciation.** I tell God what I appreciate about His presence and faithfulness in times past when He has shown Himself faithful to me.

Visit the *Chris Coursey - THRIVE channel* on YouTube for a demonstration by Dr. Jim Wilder.

Note: *The inability to restore relational circuit functions is a sign that healing is needed.*

# Day Two

Initially, joy smiles may feel awkward but once you get the hang of it, look out! Joy smiles can make you feel like you are falling in love all over again. Use your face to convey joy and delight over your spouse. We will use joy smiles throughout our time together with the hope that, by the final week, you will eagerly anticipate and crave the opportunity to build joy with your spouse.

## Joy Smiles With Music

1. Warm up your relational circuits.
2. Sitting knee to knee, take 3 minutes for joy smiles with your favorite music in the background. No talking. (*Refer to page 14.*)
3. Discuss how you experienced the exercise.
4. Did the music help create an atmosphere of joy or was it distracting?
    a. Would different music make a difference?
5. Practice five minutes of heart to heart quieting. (*Refer to page 15 for details.*)

6. Discuss how your body feels after quieting.
7. What do you prefer, the joy building or the quieting?

**Bonus 1:**

- Ask Jesus to give you an impression for the joy He feels toward your spouse and use this image as your appreciation step before starting joy.

**Bonus 2:**

- Try the exercise again only this time continue several more minutes then notice how you feel.

**Bonus 3:**

- Let your face light up and kiss your spouse like you did the first months of your marriage.

## Additional Information:

The important rule of thumb for this exercise is to notice when you feel the need to look away either because you need a break or you perceive your spouse can use a breather. This is not a stare-down contest so do your best to stay sensitive to nonverbal cues. Let your face show the joy you feel being with your beloved.

## Chris and Jen Thoughts:

*Normally we recommend you avoid trying joy smiles when you are extremely tired, but we broke our own rule for this one. On the day of practice we woke up early in the morning to drive over 12 hours to return home from vacation. Chris had recently sprained his back and was feeling much pain; however, we did not want to miss the opportunity to practice our exercises. We were pleasantly surprised to discover that even though we were tired, we were able to enjoy building joy together. Our interaction was a much lower energy state than usual, so we found ourselves taking longer rests in between joyful glances.*

*In spite of this, we walked away feeling refreshed and rejuvenated.*

## Additional Resources:

- *Joy Starts Here* at www.joystartshere.com
- *Jesus In Mind Talks*, Volume 3 at www.joystartshere.com
- Connexus for a thriving community at www.joystartshere.com
- *THRIVE Training* at www.thrivetoday.org
- *Outsmarting Yourself* by Dr. Karl and Charlotte Lehman
    - www.kclehman.com, www.outsmartingyourself.org, www.immanuelapproach.com
- *Living from the Heart Jesus Gave You* at www.joystartshere.com
- *The Complete Guide to Living with Men* by E. James Wilder at www.joystartshere.com
- *THRIVE 52-week Skill Guides* at www.thrivetoday.org
- *THRIVE-at-Home* Online Curriculum at www.thrivetoday.org

## *DAY 2 NOTES - THOUGHTS - OBSERVATIONS:*

# Joy Smiles

One of the delightful exercises you practice throughout the *Thirty Days of JOY* handbook involves using your eyes and face to build joy with your spouse. Sounds easy, doesn't it? Joy smiles describe what happens when you look at your spouse and convey, *I am so glad to be with you!* You grow joy, you look away to rest, then you start all over again. A joy expression means your face lights up as your eyes twinkle. Before you know it, a wide grin appears. All of these signals are mirrored on your spouse's face.

Joy is a high-energy state for the brain. Eye contact allows for the speedy transmission of right hemisphere to right hemisphere signals between two people, which alternate back and forth at six cycles per second. This cycle amplifies joy. A high-joy state makes you feel seen, loved and special. While the theory is too comprehensive to go into much detail here, the point we want you to walk away with is that face to face contact provides the best platform for you and your spouse to start and sustain joy. This joy exercise is nonverbal so practice using your face to convey what you feel rather than words.

If you are in tune with your partner and synchronized, you will discover that it does not take very long before you need to rest, and that is fine. You may feel the urge to break eye contact after only a few seconds. Breaking eye contact lets you 'catch your breath' to rest and recharge. Once you feel refreshed you can start all over again, building and growing more joy. You will have plenty of opportunities to practice this exercise. While it may feel awkward at first, keep practicing and you will discover that practice makes a big difference in your comfort levels. Soon you'll be having fun while you train your brain and bond with some serious joy!

# Heart To Heart Holding

One of the refreshing ways you rest with your spouse in the *Thirty Days of JOY* handbook involves a fun little exercise we call "Heart to Heart Holding" based on research that shows when couples are close together in proximity their breathing and heart rates synchronize.[1] Studies show that heart rates between bonded couples beat in synch after gazing into each other's eyes and this can happen when two people work together on a task and they trust each other.[2] This means as you hold your beloved your hearts begin to synchronize during those cuddly moments. Thanks to the bonding hormone oxytocin you get even more bang for your buck as oxytocin levels increase as people hold each other. You should feel calm, connected and peaceful.

To achieve the most benefit from this exercise, position your bodies so that your hearts (behind and left of your breastbone) are as close to each other as possible, such as chest to back, or chest to chest holding. Soon you and your spouse will have beating hearts that are in synch. You should feel relaxed, calm and peaceful.

1 http://www.ncbi.nlm.nih.gov/pubmed/21910541 and http://www.ncbi.nlm.nih.gov/pubmed/23107993

2 http://sciencenordic.com/trust-makes-our-hearts-beat-one

# Day Three

Appreciation is a foundational element we will use throughout this handbook. A little appreciation goes a long way. Appreciation turns around a sour mood, a bad day and a frustrating interaction. You may notice appreciation helps you warm up your relational circuits to shine even brighter. Appreciation diffuses stress, brings peace and creates a sunny smile on your face. It is especially fun when you can appreciate your spouse and your special shared memories together.

## Appreciation Exercise

1. Warm up your relational circuits.
2. Remember as many details as you can from your wedding day that brought you joy.
    a. If you like, find and view pictures or video footage from your wedding day.
3. Share these moments, conversations and pictures with your spouse.
4. Take turns retelling the story of your special day with as many details as you can remember.
5. Notice how you are feeling and express this to your spouse.

**Bonus 1:**

- Invite Immanuel to show you where He was during your wedding day. Ask what expression was on His face as you 'tied the knot.'

**Bonus 2:**

- Breathe deeply while doing heart to heart holding and kiss your spouse.

**Bonus 3:**

- Try the exercise again and reflect on meaningful aspects from your honeymoon.

## Chris and Jen Thoughts:

*We frequently practice appreciation to move us into relational mode and improve our moods and interactions. When we tried this specific exercise it was great fun! We felt refreshed, peaceful and joyful after remembering and sharing our appreciation memories and I (Jen) had an especially meaningful Immanuel moment when I asked Jesus where He was and what expression was on His face during our wedding day. I felt like He said He was proudly walking me down the aisle and entrusting me to the care of the special man He picked just for me. It left me (and Chris when I shared this with him) feeling special, seen and loved.*

## Additional Resources:

- *Joy Starts Here* at www.joystartshere.com
- *Jesus In Mind* Talks, Volume 3 and 17 at www.joystartshere.com
- *Share Immanuel* booklet at www.joystartshere.com
- Connexus for a thriving community at www.joystartshere.com
- *THRIVE Training* at www.thrivetoday.org
- *Outsmarting Yourself* by Dr. Karl and Charlotte Lehman
    - www.kclehman.com, www.outsmartingyourself.org, www.immanuelapproach.com
- *Living From The Heart Jesus Gave You* at www.joystartshere.com
- *THRIVE 52-week Skill Guides* at www.thrivetoday.org
- *The Complete Guide to Living with Men* by E. James Wilder at www.joystartshere.com

## *DAY 3 NOTES - THOUGHTS - OBSERVATIONS:*

# Day Four

Food and mealtime is an excellent way to bond. The Bible frequently mentions food-related activities and fellowship meals. We want to create opportunities to start joy using food and interaction with your spouse. You may have heard the saying "the best way to a man's heart is through his stomach," and this is because people bond through food, especially food from someone special. More than eating food alone, God created us to bond *with the people who feed us.* This pattern glues us to the people who satisfy and nourish us. Our goal is to enjoy each other in playful ways using food as the fuel for fun.

## Feeding, Fun And Food

1. Take a moment to warm up your relational circuits.
2. Take turns feeding each other a meal, snack or dessert. Yes, this will probably feel awkward, but have fun and laugh. Try not to spill or drop food on each other.
3. While you feed each other express how you feel your spouse

feeds you spiritually, emotionally, mentally, physically and relationally.
4. When finished, discuss ways you can better "feed" your spouse.

**Bonus 1:**

- Thank Jesus for your spouse so your spouse can hear.

**Bonus 2:**

- List some of the ways that God "feeds" you and your family. Bless Jesus for the ways He feeds and provides for you and your family.

## Chris and Jen Thoughts:

*We found this exercise significant, especially the bonus step where we take turns thanking Jesus for our spouse. This step warmed me (Jen) with appreciation and put smiles on both of our faces. We felt seen and cherished. For the exercise we practiced feeding each other with cheese and crackers; this proved to be a light snack that was enjoyable and tasty. It was fun to come up with a list of different ways we feed each other. Chris enjoyed the challenge of finding better ways to feed me while I enjoyed hearing Chris thank Jesus for me. The exercise ran smoothly and quickly; this was a worthwhile activity.*

*At the end we both concluded, "We need to do this more often!"*

## Additional Resources:

- *Joy Starts Here* at www.joystartshere.com
- *Jesus In Mind* Talks, Volume 15 and 28 at www.joystartshere.com
- *The Complete Guide to Living with Men* by E. James Wilder at www.joystartshere.com

## *DAY 4 NOTES - THOUGHTS - OBSERVATIONS:*

# Day Five

For many of us, family and community were not very effective at training us to recognize and respect overwhelm cues. In spite of this absence, overwhelm recognition plays an important role in developing the joy and safety we need and want for our marriages. It is all too common to miss overwhelm cues until someone starts crying, reacting or withdrawing.

Warning signals for overwhelm are crying, laughing, pulling back, breaking eye contact, muscle tension/stiff body, shallow breathing and fearful racing thoughts of "I want this to stop."

The goal of this exercise is to help you start to notice overwhelm cues, and learn the importance of respecting these cues in your spouse in order to keep joy levels higher than anxiety and distress. Overwhelm recognition is a skill that creates security and safety. Let's face it, we enjoy feeling protected and cared for by our spouse!

## Overwhelm – *When To Disengage*

1. Warm up your relational circuits.
2. Turn on a music device (phone, stereo or television) that increases in volume. After choosing who will start, one of you slowly turn up the music while looking for non-verbal overwhelm cues on your partner's face and body. Once you observe an overwhelm cue, reduce the volume. Slowly raise the music volume again until you identify overwhelm cues in your spouse then reduce the music volume. Repeat cycle until the song finishes.
3. Discuss what you noticed and ask your spouse how well you respected his/her overwhelm cues.
4. Repeat Step 2 in new roles.
5. Discuss the exercise.
    a. Who had an easier time recognizing overwhelm cues?
    b. How can you better respect overwhelm levels in your relationship?
6. Take a few minutes of heart to heart quieting.

**Bonus 1:**

- Discuss how strong or weak your parents were in terms of staying relational when they felt overwhelmed.

**Bonus 2:**

- Take turns discussing what you learned about how you overwhelm your spouse and what the consequences are when you push past his/her limits.

## Additional Information:

The focus of this exercise is to keep the attention on how well you respected his/her overwhelm cues and not how your spouse fails to recognize your cues. If either of you starts to feel "stuck" or triggered while discussing overwhelm, one helpful troubleshooting step is to invite Jesus to share how He would respond to overwhelm moments when you or your spouse feels maxed and vulnerable. Immanuel respects our limits and knows what we need, so it is helpful to look to Him for guidance and input into these moments. *Remember, when people do not respect our limits it is annoying at the least, and painful at the most. Do not be surprised if you notice strong reactions that need to be quieted.*

## Chris and Jen Thoughts:

*This proved to be another insightful exercise. We used an iPhone to play music and we both picked a music style that the other did not care for very much in order to "enhance" the experience. We unfortunately picked longer songs which, in retrospect, was not helpful. We suggest songs that are three minutes max. We not only turned up the volume but moved the device closer to our spouse's face as we increased volume levels then moved the device away from our partner as we decreased the volume. I, Chris, noticed that I started to feel annoyed during the brief moments when Jen was slow to pick up my overwhelm signals. This response reminded me that my relational circuits were dimming; however, once she picked up the cues and quickly moved the phone away from my face (and turned down the volume) I felt respected and cared for. Our reactions were fascinating for both of us!*

*The discussion was also beneficial as we examined patterns in our lives and steps we both can take in order to better respect overwhelm levels and moments when the other feels overwhelmed.*

## Additional Resources:

- *Joy Starts Here* at www.joystartshere.com
- *Jesus In Mind* Talks, Volume 8 at www.joystartshere.com
- *Belonging* module in the Connexus for a thriving community at www.joystartshere.com
- *THRIVE Training* at www.thrivetoday.org
    - *Joy Rekindled* Marriage Retreats
    - Training Tracks I, II and III
    - *THRIVE 52-week Skill Guides*
- *The Complete Guide to Living with Men* by E. James Wilder at www.joystartshere.com
- *Outsmarting Yourself* by Dr. Karl and Charlotte Lehman
    - www.kclehman.com, www.outsmartingyourself.org, www.immanuelapproach.com

## *DAY 5 NOTES - THOUGHTS - OBSERVATIONS:*

# Day Six

Most of us live with varying degrees of tension in our bodies. Sometimes we simply do not recognize it or we don't know how to alleviate the tension or stress we feel. You might catch a glimpse of your body's tension by the end of the day when you sink into your chair and take your first deep breath.

Unless we are in pain, many of us tune out the specific signals our body is sending us concerning fatigue and tension. We are used to "pushing through it." In this exercise we not only want you to relax your body but notice *how your body feels*. As an added insight, Level 4 of your brain's control center has to be active and synchronized to effectively assess what your body is feeling. Level 4 is the creative region of your brain where your identity, or *who you know yourself to be*, is stored. As you begin to pay attention to how you feel in your body, your sense of *what is important* and how to express the best of yourself according to personal preference and values starts to develop with clarity.

## Getting Prefrontal

1. Warm up your relational circuits.
2. Mentally scan your body. Where do you feel tense, stiff or tired?
3. Tighten then relax that specific part of your body. Do this for a few minutes until you begin to feel some relief.
4. Next, lay on the floor with your hand on your belly. Breathe from your belly and watch your hand go up and down as you inhale and exhale.
5. Practice three minutes of joy smiles.
6. Notice what changed in your body with each step. Discuss how you feel after some practice with quiet and joy.
7. Close the exercise by praying together using a voice tone that calms and relaxes.

**Bonus:**

- Take a hot bath or shower (individually or together) to better help your body relax.

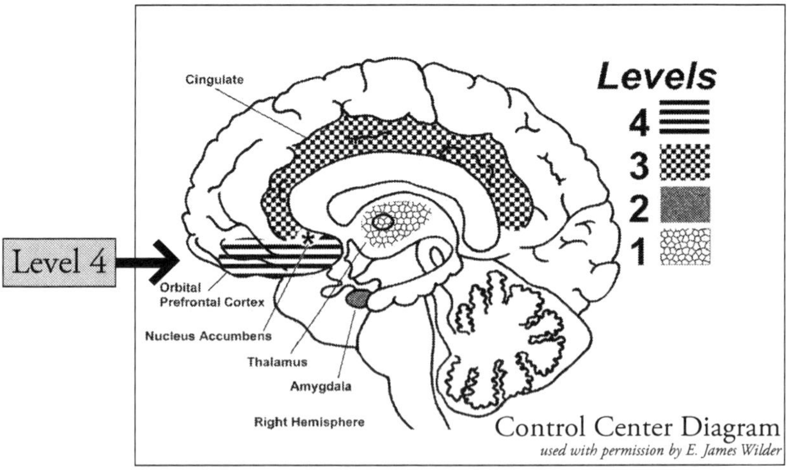

Control Center Diagram
*used with permission by E. James Wilder*

## Chris and Jen Thoughts:

*I, Chris, must confess I did not want to do this exercise. On our designated night for practice, I just finished a long day of work and Jen was preparing to go out for the evening. The boys were with grandma, and I was in the middle of heating up a frozen pizza for my low-key, restful evening. Jen had just enough time for us to do the exercise, but I felt rushed and noticed I was feeling some resistance to Jen's invitation to start the exercise. My thoughts were, "Oh, let's skip it tonight and we'll catch up tomorrow night." At one point I even said, "But my pizza will get cold by the time we are finished." I was obviously looking for an escape route. Jen kindly responded with, "Honey, it may help if you warm up your relational circuits first." She was right; I was hungry, tired and, well, non-relational in that particular moment. After a few moments practicing the relational circuit exercises, I felt my motivation increase and my energy return, so we practiced the exercise. I realized that my body was feeling tense, I needed some quieting and I definitely needed some joy! By the end of the exercise I felt relaxed, recharged and refreshed. I was glad we did the exercise as I would have missed out on a very special connection with my wife. I then enjoyed my pizza in a relational place that made the evening much more satisfying.*

*This far in the sequence of exercises I am noticing a large difference in my joy levels and I feel more relational with my wife and sons. I look forward to the rest of the exercises because they are certainly paying off for me. I hope the above example will encourage all of you because, like me, you will come up with numerous reasons why you don't have the time, energy or desire to do an exercise on a certain day, but I encourage you to get relational and go for it. The rewards far outweigh the cost.*

## Additional Resources:

- *Jesus In Mind* Talks, Volume 8, 10 and 19 at www.joystartshere.com
- Connexus for a thriving community at www.joystartshere.com
- *THRIVE Training* at www.thrivetoday.org
    - *Joy Rekindled* Marriage Retreats
    - Training Tracks I, II and III
    - THRIVE 52-week Skill Guides
- *The Complete Guide to Living with Men* by E. James Wilder at www.joystartshere.com
- *Living From The Heart Jesus Gave You* at www.joystartshere.com

## *DAY 6 NOTES - THOUGHTS - OBSERVATIONS:*

# Day Seven

We do well to pay attention to our relational circuits in order to function at our best relationally. Where else would we want to be our best than with the people we live with? With practice we can improve our ability to notice when our relational circuits start to dim then quickly warm them up again. Once this becomes a habit or pattern, we can minimize the "non-relational" casualties that happen in our home. Additionally there is this remarkable connection between relational circuits being dimmed that leads to an increase in cravings. In our house, we notice a clear pattern when our relational circuits go dim our cravings for ice cream increase. When we are unable to remove ice cream thoughts from our minds we know it's time to restore our RC's!

## Relational Circuits And Cravings

1. Use the RC checklist on page 6 to see if your relational circuits are warmed up and on.
2. If you feel non-relational, practice getting your relational circuits

on using one of the *Shalom My Body* exercises or by remembering appreciation (*Refer to page 6 for details*).

3. Discuss:
    a. When in the past week have you noticed your relational circuits were on?
    b. Have you been able to recognize when they were dimmed or off? Have you been able to practice getting your relational circuits on again?
    c. What happens in your thoughts when your relational circuits are off or dimmed?
    d. When your relational circuits are off or dimmed what cravings (BEEPS) do you desire and turn to for comfort? (BEEPS are *Behaviors, Experiences, Events, People and Substances* we rely on for relief and to artificially regulate our emotions.)
4. Tell a story about a special shared memory that makes you smile.
5. After telling your stories go through the RC checklist again. Check for any changes to your relational circuits.

**Bonus:**

- Practice heart to heart quieting on page 15 and synchronize your breathing. When you finish, pray together and invite Immanuel to cover you with His blanket of peace and ask for His character to be expressed in your marriage.

## Additional Information:

It is worth noting that when you are in a non-relational mode you may have little desire to turn your relational circuits back on again. This is common. Additionally, if a relationship is painful or frustrating, relational circuits tend to go off and stay off, and getting them on again can make you more aware of pain. The good news is that you can disarm and process pain much more effectively when your

RC's are on compared to when they are dimmed or off. Keeping them off does not fix your pain but hinders you from effectively processing your pain. When you notice your RC's are off and you are resistant to the very notion of getting yourself back into relational mode, your challenge is to practice getting them on again and notice the changes. *You have more relational resources to deal with pain and problems when you are in relational mode.* You are able to perceive Immanuel's presence when your relational circuits are on, which is always a game-changer for problems and pain.

## Chris and Jen Thoughts:

*Jen and I (Chris) practiced this exercise just before bed. We were both feeling tired after another busy day, but once we started the exercise, I enjoyed the chance to review my week and highlight moments my RC's were on and moments they were off. During the review I told Jen a short but meaningful Immanuel "thought" I had the day before during prayer about how I felt Immanuel met me in a personal, loving way which left me feeling seen and comforted. From then on I experienced a significant increase in my relational circuits for the rest of the day and into the next day. After we told our special shared memories at the end, we both noticed a difference in how we felt. We were more peaceful, joyful and relaxed. The story was a refreshing way to finish the exercise and end our day.*

## Additional Resources:

- *Jesus In Mind* Talks, Volume 8, 10, 15, 22 and 28 at www.joystartshere.com
- Connexus for a thriving community at www.joystartshere.com
- *THRIVE Training* at www.thrivetoday.org
    - o *Joy Rekindled* Marriage Retreats
    - o Training Tracks I, II and III
    - o THRIVE 52-week Skill Guides
- *The Complete Guide to Living with Men* by E. James Wilder at www.joystartshere.com
- *Outsmarting Yourself* by Dr. Karl and Charlotte Lehman
    - o www.kclehman.com, www.outsmartingyourself.org, www.immanuelapproach.com

## *DAY 7 NOTES - THOUGHTS - OBSERVATIONS:*

# Day Eight

As mentioned before, you will find several opportunities for joy and quiet throughout this handbook as these two energy states make up your natural rhythms. As you alternate and share times of joy and quiet with your spouse you will grow a deeper, richer bond. You will feel refreshed. We hope you will crave genuine joy and rest as you work your way toward the finish line of this handbook.

## Joy Smiles Without Music

1. Warm up your relational circuits.
2. Ask Jesus to give you an impression regarding the joy He feels toward your spouse and use this image as your appreciation step before starting joy.
3. Take three minutes for joy smiles without music in the background. Refer to page 14 if needed.
4. Discuss what this exercise felt like.
5. Did the silence create a better atmosphere for joy?

6. Practice five minutes of heart to heart holding on page 15.
7. Discuss how your body feels after quieting.
8. Which do you prefer - the joy building or the quieting?

**Bonus 1:**

- Try the exercise again only this time around add several more minutes to your joy smile practice, then notice how you feel.

**Bonus 2:**

- Let your face light up and kiss your spouse like you did the first months of your marriage.

## Chris and Jen Thoughts:

*I, Jen, enjoyed doing this exercise, especially the step of asking Jesus for an impression of His joy towards my spouse. When I asked Immanuel, a remarkable image came to mind where I saw Jesus with His hands on Chris' shoulders proudly delighting over him. This picture made me smile. :)*

*I, Chris, noticed what I felt was an Immanuel-inspired image that added to my joy as well. With these images in mind we were able to hit higher joy levels than previous times we have practiced the joy smiles. We enjoyed the refreshing combination of joy and quiet!*

## Additional Resources:

- *Jesus In Mind* Talks, Volume 3 and 12 at www.joystartshere.com
- *Share Immanuel* booklet at www.joystartshere.com
- Connexus for a thriving community at www.joystartshere.com
- *THRIVE Training* at www.thrivetoday.org
    - *Joy Rekindled* Marriage Retreats
    - Training Tracks I, II and III
    - THRIVE 52-week Skill Guides
- *The Complete Guide to Living with Men* by E. James Wilder at www.joystartshere.com
- *Outsmarting Yourself* by Dr. Karl and Charlotte Lehman
    - www.kclehman.com, www.outsmartingyourself.org, www.immanuelapproach.com

## *DAY 8 NOTES - THOUGHTS - OBSERVATIONS:*

# Day Nine

Jesus is always with us. While Scripture is clear about this truth, our experience tends to be a bit more fuzzy. For many of us it is rare that we keep an ongoing awareness of God's closeness much less know where Immanuel is as it relates to us in good and hard times. Pain, fatigue, overwhelm, fear, anger and more make the Immanuel Lifestyle difficult. We hope this handbook introduces something new and fresh for your relationship with the King of Kings.

For *Day Nine* we practice perceiving Jesus' presence in a way that leaves us feeling special, seen and comforted. Noticing Immanuel's gentle presence works best for our nervous system when we start by *remembering appreciation*, something or someone that brings us joy and is a gift from God, or practicing an *interactive memory,* where we remember a time we felt seen by God as though He was right there interacting with us. When we mentally return to the Immanuel memory we are delighted to discover He is there. We can *interact.* Both states, *appreciation* and *interactive memories*, place our brain in the best possible state to perceive God's presence. As followers of the King we can practice this as a lifestyle.

## Immanuel Practice

1. Warm up your relational circuits.
2. Take turns telling appreciation with God stories where you felt like God answered a prayer. Include a story about a time you felt like God was with you. Notice how this step feels in your body.
3. Focus on one of your interactive or appreciation memories until you start to feel peaceful shalom in your mind and body.
4. As you remember your appreciation memory or notice the awareness of Immanuel's presence with you, invite Immanuel to share what is on His mind for you today.
5. Notice what thoughts come to mind. Any time you feel distracted return to your appreciation or interactive memory until you feel shalom once again. Continue to dialogue with Immanuel and notice what thoughts come to mind.
6. Discuss how these practice steps went for you. Did you notice any thoughts that could have been Immanuel's thoughts?
7. Review the *Day Ten* exercise since some preparation is required.

**Bonus:**

- If you get stuck at any point in the exercise, tell more appreciation stories along with stories where you feel like God answered prayers throughout your life. These stories will help as you practice the rest of the exercise, especially if you have a difficult time connecting and perceiving Immanuel's presence.

## Chris and Jen Thoughts:

*This exercise was a very refreshing activity for us right before bed. We work hard to make Immanuel practice a regular exercise in our marriage and much to our surprise, we had a difficult time remembering answered prayer moments on Step 2. Step 3 was actually easier and this was surprising to me (Jen) because I used to feel that I could not hear from God and trying to listen and perceive God's active presence created much inner turmoil for me. It is now much easier for me to remember times I felt close and interactive with Immanuel, and this is a monumental answer to prayer!*

*I hope this gives you encouragement, especially if you can relate to my struggle. Practice and prayer does pay off.*

## Additional Resources:

- *Joyful Journey* book at www.joystartshere.com
- *Share Immanuel* booklet at www.joystartshere.com
- *Jesus In Mind* Talks, Volume 12 and 20 at www.joystartshere.com
- *Immanuel: Taking Healing to the World* CD at www.joystartshere.com
- *2011 Share Immanuel Evening Sessions* CD at www.joystartshere.com
- Connexus for a thriving community at www.joystartshere.com
- *THRIVE Training* at www.thrivetoday.org
    - *Joy Rekindled* Marriage Retreats
    - Training Tracks I, II and III
    - THRIVE 52-week Skill Guides
- *Outsmarting Yourself* by Dr. Karl and Charlotte Lehman
    - www.kclehman.com, www.outsmartingyourself.org, www.immanuelapproach.com

## *DAY 9 NOTES - THOUGHTS - OBSERVATIONS:*

# Day Ten

It is fun to do something special for your spouse. With a little creativity you can bless him or her with a gift without spending a cent. Some thought and planning makes your gift even more special and meaningful. Here is your chance to creatively share your love.

## Love On Your Spouse

1. Warm up your relational circuits.
2. Find a small gift your spouse would enjoy without spending money. (*Be creative: Cook or grill a special meal, pick wildflowers, make a gift, frame a picture, give a massage, etc.*)
3. Discuss how it feels to give and receive these heartfelt gifts.
4. Notice if your attachment light comes on in response to giving or receiving a gift from your spouse. (*See pages 64-67 if attachment lights are unfamiliar to you.*)
5. Share with your partner what you appreciate about his or her heart. (*What are you thankful for as it relates to your partner?*)
6. Practice heart to heart holding.

**Bonus:**

- Discuss what makes your spouse feel loved and special. Is it having your attention, hearing how much you love him or her, enjoying time together, etc. Example: "I notice you feel loved when I greet you with a smile and kiss. You feel loved when I do the dishes…"

## Chris and Jen Thoughts:

*I, Jen, love sharing what I appreciate about Chris' heart and, of course, hearing what he appreciates about me. I feel secure and treasured as I listen to Chris express the qualities he appreciates about my heart.*

*Jen and I (Chris) enjoyed the little bit of planning involved for this particular exercise because on this day we took our boys swimming in the afternoon and it pushed our schedule back enough that our normal routine was interrupted. While we were able to feed the boys dinner, Jen and I did not have a chance to eat. Once the boys were down for bed, Jen graciously offered to make me whatever meal I wanted. She created a "wonderfully yummy" omelet that was absolutely delicious to my taste buds. We were able to interact without interruptions during the meal, which made it even more special. I felt taken care of by her gift. My small gift to Jen was a back massage which helped her relax after a tense day. We found the appreciation step meaningful and enjoyed closing the exercise with the quieting step. This prepared us for bed. While our joy levels were pretty good before, we continue to notice a difference in our joy as we practice these exercises. Momentum is heading in the right direction.*

## Additional Resources:

- *Jesus In Mind* Talks, Volume 13 at www.joystartshere.com
- Connexus for a thriving community at www.joystartshere.com
- *THRIVE Training* at www.thrivetoday.org
    - *Joy Rekindled* Marriage Retreats
    - Training Tracks I, II and III
    - THRIVE 52-week Skill Guides
- *The Complete Guide to Living with Men* by E. James Wilder at www.joystartshere.com
- *Outsmarting Yourself* by Dr. Karl and Charlotte Lehman
    - www.kclehman.com, www.outsmartingyourself.org, www.immanuelapproach.com

## *DAY 10 NOTES - THOUGHTS - OBSERVATIONS:*

# Clarity Regarding Relational Circuits And Attachment Light

The handbook you are holding is designed to increase your joy and accomplish several significant action steps for your marriage. Two particular steps are worth their weight in gold. You will practice training your brain's relational circuits and you will learn to synchronize "attachment lights." This means you both feel connected, seen, valued, enjoyed and loved in mutuality. You feel as though you are on the same page relationally. You are in synch and you feel understood. **Both steps are designed to give you the full range of joy while you connect with your spouse.** Both are worth learning about.

While the Heimlich Maneuver may look strange to the untrained eye, anyone who has choked on food and was then delivered by this life-saving technique cares little for how strange the technique appears. Rather, the person feels a deep sense of gratitude simply because it worked and they can breathe again. Some of the exercises you will practice may seem odd or strange at first; however, as you begin to breathe better relationally, you will feel satisfied with the results. For example, we use training exercises that are designed to train your brain's relational circuits. Some of these exercises may seem strange or awkward, but much like the Heimlich Maneuver, the exercise works for moving people into relational mode. Now it is time to explore more about your brain's relational circuits <u>and</u> attachment lights in order to avoid confusion about the two.

As you discovered by looking at the Relational Circuit Checklist on page 6, your brain's relational circuits should "warm up" more often and stay on even if you are not interacting with another person. Your attachment light, however, should come on *as needed* for interaction then go off as you rest. The attachment circuit of your brain (*level one of the control center*) is a different brain system and region than your relational circuits. While the difference becomes clearer with each training track of THRIVE, these two circuits are distinct with different functions that we will explore briefly.

Theoretically, your relational circuits should always be shining in the "on" position. This does not mean that you must interact every waking minute of the day, but your relational circuits can be on even if you are reading a book or watching a movie with another person. While you may be focused on the pages of the book or the drama on the television screen, you will know that your relational circuits are active and on if you still care about the feelings, thoughts and opinions of the person, even if you are not interacting at the particular moment. You feel as though the person is still important to you even if you are focused on something else. If your relational circuits are OFF you may be annoyed by their presence and feel bothered that they are sitting next to you. You do not want to interact with them nor do you care what they think or feel.

Your attachment light, however, should not be in a continual "on" or "off" state. Rather, your attachment light should activate and light up when you want to bond and desire to hug, talk, listen, grow joy, etc. Once you need to rest or take a breather your attachment light should quickly switch "off." This attachment pattern can continue on a moment by moment basis.

Having both your relational circuits and your attachment light on means you will enjoy the rich flavor of interaction and attunement with the other person. You genuinely care for them. You want to be with them. You feel the reward of interacting with them. When you feel like you have had enough interaction, your attachment light goes off and you avert your gaze to rest and "catch your breath" before more interaction ensues. Even though you are now resting, as long as your relational circuits are still on you continue to value and care about the feelings and thoughts of the other person. If your relational circuits are off, you may care very little about the other person's feelings in the moment. You may even want to say hurtful things and avoid the chance to connect, bond, talk or interact. At this point any interaction becomes more about your wants, your desires and your needs. You may not feel much concern for what the other person is thinking, feeling or experiencing. These are moments relational casualties happen.

There is some overlap between the two circuits, which means in "live time interactions" attunement and nonverbal communication runs much faster than we can consciously keep track of so it's much harder to catch in the moment. "Are my relational circuits on?" "Is my attachment light on?" With practice you can begin to observe this phenomena with more clarity both in yourself and in other people. The advantage for knowing what you have available at any given moment means you can jumpstart and shift into a more relational mode which gives you *more resources to navigate relational interactions*. Trying to drive a car with a dead battery just does not go very well. A jumpstart makes everything better.

We see this dynamic clearer in a two-month old baby who wants mommy. Baby will cry and scream for mommy because she only wants mommy; no one else will do. Her relational circuits are off (*and undeveloped at this stage*); however her attachment light is on for the one and only person in the world she wants: MOMMY! She wants only mommy and cares very little about anything else in the moment. Baby intensely wants mommy and will throw a non-relational fit to achieve her goal: mommy.

Take a look at the adjacent diagram to better understand attachment styles. You can learn more about relational circuits and attachment light phenomena through training and resources at www.joystartshere.com, and the thorough resources of Karl Lehman M.D. at www.kclehman.com.

# Attachment Styles

Non-Secure Attachment:

## DISMISSIVE

**ATTACHMENT LIGHT OFF**

My parent/caregiver was rarely emotionally available and my needs, wants, preferences & dreams were dismissed or minimized.

I couldn't expect connection, so I live life on my own. I stay distant, avoidant & withdrawn as a coping strategy.

I might be highly competent or a workaholic. I operate from duty – not from joy.

I may appear uncaring & unavailable; dismissing the importance of emotions & relationships.

Life is safer and feels better alone & undisturbed.

**ATTACHMENT LIGHTS GO ON & OFF TOGETHER**

We are designed to be completely fulfilled only in joyful, secure relationships with God & each other.

When my attachments are secure, my life is powered by joy.

- We have high joy capacity
- We can synchronize with each other in rhythms of joy & quiet together
- We can intimately bond & work together in joy for life
- We have inner confidence to engage with the world
- We can fulfill our purpose & destiny together

Non-Secure Attachment:

## DISORGANIZED

**ATTACHMENT LIGHT ON & OFF**

My relationship with my parent/caregiver was the source of both comfort and terror. I was so afraid of the chaotic/disorganized behavior that I found it impossible to be calmed. I couldn't make sense of the "come here – go away" relationship. So I grew up continually afraid.

I want to attach but at the same time I am terrified, as I am driven to attach to the ones who hurt me.

If I feel needed or asked to attach in anyway, I will be triggered into fear. My fear can explode into rage for no apparent reason.

Relationships are difficult for me as I can be hostile, controlling and aggressive. My unregulated emotions may be followed by withdrawal to protect myself from pain.

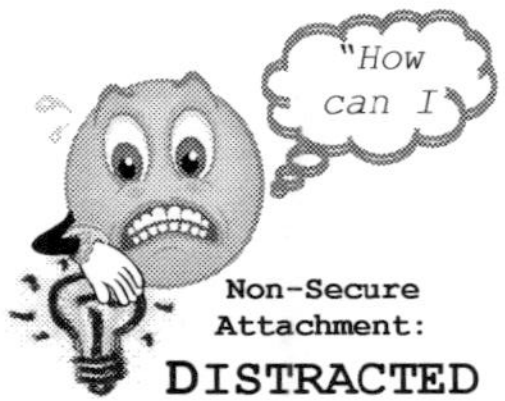


Non-Secure Attachment:

## DISTRACTED

**ATTACHMENT LIGHT ON**

My parent/caregiver sent mixed signals about attachment. Our interactions were based on my parent's needs, not mine, & were often intrusive.

Since I never knew if my needs would be met, I've become preoccupied with attachment.

I am highly needy, dependent & anxious, focusing on receiving comfort for my distress.

I can quickly "attach" in high energy relationships & appear quite functional – then I overwhelm you.

I may use "neediness" or distress to manipulate you for attention.

I have frequent highly emotional displays with one crisis after another.

***If my attachment is broken or not secure, I will attach to someone or something to make the pain stop.***

# Day Eleven

Four-plus stories are an amazing tool because they train the five levels of the brain to synchronize and work together. (Four levels in the right hemisphere 'plus' the left hemisphere. This means cohesive stories flow as our words match our feelings.) Four-plus stories allow us to train others (like our children) by giving an example (picture story) of what it looks like to return to joy, be joyful, and act like the people God created us to be in different emotions and situations as well as a host of other skills. These stories allow listeners to step into our shoes as we tell the story of an experience. Here is your chance to increase joy and share your stories.

## Joy Stories

1. Warm up your relational circuits.
2. Think of a joyful memory with your spouse from the past year.
3. Summarize your story on the 4+ story sheet (see page 72).
4. Take turns sharing your stories with your spouse. Use the four-plus story elements.

5. Discuss with your spouse:
    a. What do you notice while telling or listening to joy stories?
    b. Did you notice any changes before, during or after the story?
6. Be prepared to do tomorrow's exercise during a mealtime. (Oh, will you have fun!)

**Bonus 1:**

- Practice one of the joy smile exercises with or without music. Discuss what you have noticed about your relational circuits.

**Bonus 2:**

- Let your face light up and kiss your spouse like you did the first months of your marriage.

## Additional Information:

Use your four-plus story sheet on page 72 as your guide for the joy story. Include the story elements that will make your joy story a home run. The better you convey the emotion the more impact your story will have.

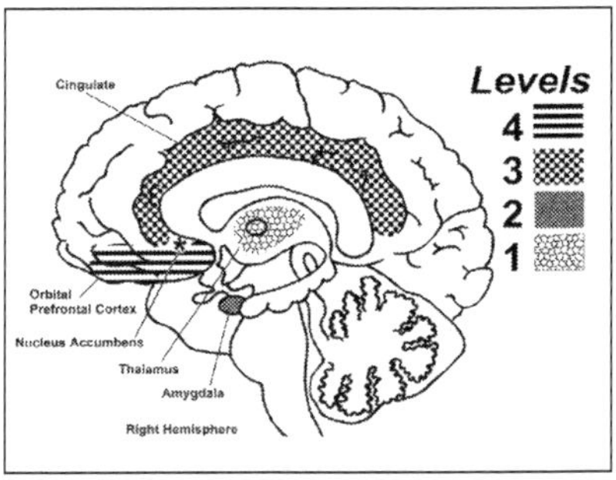


Control Center Diagram
*Used with permission by E. James Wilder*

## Additional Resources:

- *Jesus In Mind* Talks, Volume 3, 5, 7 and 10 at www.joystartshere.com
- Connexus for a thriving community at www.joystartshere.com
- *THRIVE Training* at www.thrivetoday.org
    - o *Joy Rekindled* Marriage Retreats
    - o Training Tracks I, II and III
    - o THRIVE 52-week Skill Guides

## Chris and Jen Thoughts:

*Chris and I were preparing to start our exercise in the evening when, after putting the boys to bed, our three year old did something dangerous in his room that scared and upset me. Once he was settled in bed, it was difficult for me to quiet. My heart was still racing and my adrenaline was surging. My relational circuits were clearly off. Chris and I started the exercise by warming up our relational circuits (which, again, were pretty well off for me in the moment) then we practiced our joy stories. It was refreshing how the relational circuit exercise and the joy stories helped me calm down and shift back into relational mode. I find it satisfying to see the training work in live time!*

# THRIVE Four-Plus Story Worksheet

## Preparation checklist

1. This story has a moderate feeling level and is not too intense □
2. I have told this story before □
3. I do not need to be guarded in telling this story □
4. This story is autobiographical (I am involved in the story) □
5. This story illustrates a specific feeling □

## Write out ideas for the following parts of your 4+ story

6. Briefly describe the situation

7. List feeling words for this story

8. During this story my body felt:

9. The things I did in this story that demonstrate how I like to act in this emotion are:
(*If I did not act like myself at the time, I now would have liked to have done this.*)

## Follow-up checklist

- I showed the authentic emotion on my face and in my voice □
- I maintained eye contact while storytelling □
- I used feeling words for my emotions □
- I used feeling words for my body sensations □
- I told the story like I was involved (autobiographical) □
- I kept my story concise □

## *DAY 11 NOTES - THOUGHTS - OBSERVATIONS:*

# Day Twelve

Our boys enjoy the opportunity to "sing to Jesus" before each meal. In fact, if we forget to sing our prayer to Jesus before meals, our three-year old earnestly reminds us we "neeeed to siiiinnnnggg to Jeeesuuussss!" Every time we join hands around the table and prepare to sing, our eighteen-month old grows a wide smile on his face as he eagerly reaches for a hand. With little children at the table, mealtimes can easily turn into stressful moments. We have noticed that singing together as we invite Jesus to join us sets the tone for much more peaceful and joyful mealtimes. As we pay attention to His thoughts and exchange joyful glances, we notice a remarkable difference in each meal. We suggest every family try this!

## Cravings, Food And Bonding

1. Before eating: Pay attention to your body and notice how your cravings feel.
2. Take some time to quiet your body and your food cravings. Breathe deeply and warm up your relational circuits by remem-

bering appreciation or practicing the *Shalom My Body* exercises. (Refer to page 6 for a review.)

3. Sing the Jesus prayer with joy smiles as you hold hands and light up your face. (*Watch the Jesus prayer demonstration on YouTube at the Chris Coursey - THRIVE channel.*)
4. Invite Jesus to join your mealtime and notice any shalom-producing thoughts that come to mind during the meal.
5. Tell your spouse any possible Jesus thoughts:
    a. What is Jesus doing as it relates to you?
    b. What does Jesus appreciate and enjoy about mealtimes with your spouse and family?
6. Express appreciation with everyone at the table:
    a. Food taste and appearance.
    b. Qualities you enjoy about each other.
7. Discuss how you feel *after* the meal. What was satisfying for you? What did you most enjoy? Are you less tired? Do you feel more relational?

**Bonus 1:**

- Over family dinner time with children, have a contest to see who can come up the most aspects you appreciate from the meal including food and people.

**Bonus 2:**

- Discuss what aspects of eating and mealtime brought you joy and shalom when you were growing up. What did not bring joy and shalom? How can you use mealtimes to increase joy and shalom for you and your family/friends/community?

## Chris and Jen Thoughts:

*This special tradition started when I, Chris, was working on the Joy Starts Here book with Jim Wilder, Ed Khouri and Shelia Sutton in a cabin in Big Sky, Montana. As a group we were practicing bonding and building joy during mealtimes and Jim taught us this style of praying. When I returned from the writing trip I continued the tradition with my family, and it has become a special, meaningful and fun way to grow joy. The prayer song also helps us be relational for mealtimes. Guests enjoy learning the song as well. It is fun to watch faces light up around the table. We have the sneaky suspicion that Jesus smiles over this special act as well.*

*Chris and I (Jen) ended up doing this exercise over breakfast one morning with our boys, and it was so much fun! While we usually have fun doing our song, the added element of appreciating each family member helped me have an especially thankful perspective to start my day, and the exercise helped me delight over the boys that much more!*

## Additional Resources:

- *Joy Starts Here* book at www.joystartshere.com
- *Jesus In Mind* Talks, Volume 8, 13, 28 at www.joystartshere.com
- *Belonging* in the Connexus for a thriving community at www.joystartshere.com
- *The Complete Guide to Living with Men* by E. James Wilder at www.joystartshere.com
- *THRIVE Training* at www.thrivetoday.org
    - *Joy Rekindled* Marriage Retreats
    - Training Tracks I, II and III
    - THRIVE 52-week Skill Guides

## *DAY 12 NOTES - THOUGHTS - OBSERVATIONS:*

# Day Thirteen

Some of us Christians have a difficult time looking at our maturity level because we mistakenly equate maturity with value and self worth. Maturity may even be spiritualized or confused with physical age alone as a measurement. While the *process* of maturing is extremely important, how far along we are does not determine our value. When we were first introduced to the concept of maturity and the Life Model task lists, we immediately noticed we were very weak in the infant tasks even though we lived in adult bodies. Initially this revelation felt discouraging, but we were quickly encouraged to have a clear road map to tell us where we were stuck in our maturity and where we needed to go as a next step. For the first time we found a language and steps we could take for joyful growth.

Once we could identify areas of weakness we could explain why we repeatedly fell into the same frustrating patterns. We discovered a clear gauge to measure and understand how much we could handle without plunging into burnout. I encourage you to give this exercise an honest look. See where your strengths and weaknesses are then use this as an opportunity for growth.

For this introductory exercise you and your spouse will go through the Life Model list below and discuss how well you developed the following in your life. While it is insightful to go through this list together, you can decide what you want to do depending on your time frame.

Rate **5 to 1** with 5 the strongest, 1 the weakest. [Circle]

### Infant Tasks

5 4 3 2 1 – I have experienced strong, loving, caring bonds with mother/woman.
5 4 3 2 1 – I have experienced strong, loving, caring bonds with father/man.
5 4 3 2 1 – Important needs were met until I learned to ask.
5 4 3 2 1 – Others took the lead and synchronized with me and my feelings first.
5 4 3 2 1 – Quiet together times helped me calm myself with people around.
5 4 3 2 1 – Important people have seen me through the "eyes of heaven."
5 4 3 2 1 – I can both receive and give life.
5 4 3 2 1 – I receive with joy without guilt or shame.
5 4 3 2 1 – I can now synchronize with others and their feelings.
5 4 3 2 1 – I found people to imitate so that I now have a personality I like.
5 4 3 2 1 – I learned to regulate and quiet the following "big six" emotions:

- 5 4 3 2 1 – Anger
- 5 4 3 2 1 – Fear
- 5 4 3 2 1 – Sadness
- 5 4 3 2 1 – Disgust
- 5 4 3 2 1 – Shame
- 5 4 3 2 1 – Hopeless/despair

5 4 3 2 1 – I can return to joy from every emotion and restore broken relationships.
5 4 3 2 1 – I stay the same person over time around different people and places.
5 4 3 2 1 – I know how to rest.

### Child Tasks

5 4 3 2 1 – I can do things I don't feel like doing.
5 4 3 2 1 – I can do hard things even if they cause me some pain.
5 4 3 2 1 – I can separate my feelings, my imagination and reality in my relationships.
5 4 3 2 1 – I am comfortable with reasonable risks, attempts and failures.
5 4 3 2 1 – I have received love I did not have to earn.
5 4 3 2 1 – I know how my family came to be the way it is—family history.
5 4 3 2 1 – I know how God's family came to be the way it is.
5 4 3 2 1 – I know the "big picture" of life with the stages of maturity.
5 4 3 2 1 – I can take care of myself.

5 4 3 2 1 – I ask for what I need.
5 4 3 2 1 – I enjoy self-expression.
5 4 3 2 1 – I am growing in the things I am good at doing (personal resources and talents).
5 4 3 2 1 – I help other people to understand me better if they don't respond well to me.
5 4 3 2 1 – I have learned to control my cravings.
5 4 3 2 1 – I know what satisfies me.
5 4 3 2 1 – I see myself through the "eyes of heaven."

## Maturity Inventory

We develop maturity as we interact with God and people in multi-generational community.

1. Warm up your relational circuits.
2. What stands out in the above list as it relates to you?
3. How do your areas of weakness impact your marriage?
4. What steps can you take to strengthen areas of weakness?
5. What can you predict will hinder your efforts when you try to work on these steps?
6. What would you like to see change as you begin to expand these areas?
7. With heart-to-heart holding, take time to pray for each other.
8. Invite Immanuel to share any thoughts and ask Him to lead you to create a transformation zone.

**Bonus 1:**

- Pray for active fears that slow your maturing process.

**Bonus 2:**

- Identify unprocessed wounds that hinder you. Find resources to practice the Immanuel process for healing.

## Chris and Jen Thoughts:

*While I, Chris, have been through the maturity lists over and over throughout the years, each time I go through the list I find encouragement for the growth I have made as well as clarity for the places that require some attention. When I go through the lists, I try to think of current situations and difficulties to "gauge" myself and see where I am strong in certain areas and where I am weak. For example, on the returning to joy task, I think of current relationships that are difficult or painful and I evaluate how well I am doing in these situations. I find much encouragement working on my own maturity and it is valuable to see the training pay off for my family and community relationships. Jen and I both enjoyed this exercise, especially as we finished with some Immanuel interaction about our needs, fears and fervent desire to reach our potential in Christ. We feel encouraged to "run the race" of joyful growth in our relationship and marriage.*

## Additional Resources:

- *The Complete Guide to Living with Men* by E. James Wilder at www.joystartshere.com
- *Joy Starts Here* book at www.joystartshere.com
- *Living From The Heart Jesus Gave You* at www.joystartshere.com
- *Jesus In Mind* Talks, Volume 7, 9, 11 and 19 at www.joystartshere.com
- Connexus for a thriving community at www.joystartshere.com
- *THRIVE Training* at www.thrivetoday.org
    - o *Reach Your Potential with Joy* Maturity Retreats
    - o Training Tracks I, II and III
    - o THRIVE 52-week Skill Guides

## *DAY 13 NOTES - THOUGHTS - OBSERVATIONS:*

# Day Fourteen

Massage, assuming it is attuned, can be a sensual way to bond with your spouse. Soft touch and gentle massage can be restful and relaxing for your body. Studies show that massage lowers blood pressure while personal touch increases oxytocin levels. The added bonus of hearing your spouse express gratitude for you with a prayer of blessing can make you feel even more cozy.

## Massage

1. Warm up your relational circuits.
2. Give your spouse a ten-minute massage using the following flow and use a soft-sounding timer if needed.
    a. Spend 2 minutes in quiet.
    b. Spend 2 minutes thanking Jesus for your spouse.
    c. Spend 2 minutes in quiet.
    d. Spend 2 minutes praying a blessing over your spouse.
    e. Spend 2 minutes in quiet.

3. Now switch roles and have the massage giver become the receiver and follow the same outline as above.

**Bonus 1:**

- Practice heart to heart holding and appreciate your spouse.

**Bonus 2:**

- With heart to heart holding still in place, find aspects of your day that were particularly joyful and meaningful. Thank Jesus for your day.

## Chris and Jen Thoughts:

*We loved this exercise, especially how relaxing it was to receive a massage. We felt closer as we were able to rest and relax together. Hearing what the other was thankful for was very special and left us feeling peaceful, relaxed and cozy after this exercise. We hope you also enjoy it and feel relaxed and blessed by the end.*

## Additional Resources:

- *THRIVE Training* at www.thrivetoday.org
    - *Joy Rekindled* Marriage Retreats
    - Training Tracks I, II and III
    - THRIVE 52-week Skill Guides

## *DAY 14 NOTES - THOUGHTS - OBSERVATIONS:*

# Day Fifteen

The three elements necessary to enter the transformation zone are *1. The weak and strong interact, 2. Tender responses towards weaknesses are the rule* and *3. We return to Immanuel shalom as frequently as necessary when our peace drops out.* We want all three of these ingredients in our lives and require them in order to stay in the transformation zone where lasting change happens.

Some of us have trouble being vulnerable with our spouse and sharing our weaknesses with him or her. While there are good reasons for this resistance it can be especially hard if there is a tendency where one or both partners are critical of weakness rather than expressing tender responses when weak moments arise. In order for our marriages to be a safe place to start joy, we need to learn tender responses towards each other's weaknesses. We aim to be protectors who care for and nurture weakness opposed to predators who bite and pounce. Tenderness can be simply affirming "You sure are sleepy aren't you; what do you need right now?" after a spouse mentions, "I am tired. It's been a long day." A lack of tenderness in this moment would be, "Oh, you are not tired!" "Come on, pull it together!" or "You think you are tired; let me tell you about my day then we'll see who is tired!"

## Strength And Weakness

1. Warm up your relational circuits.
2. Think about your strengths and weaknesses in your relationship with your spouse. Where do you feel weak? Where do you feel strong? Examples:
    a. I feel weak in my ability to communicate my needs when I'm tired.
    b. I feel strong in how I attune with you in your upset.
    c. I feel weaker when it comes to being playful.
    d. I feel weak in how I protect our time.
    e. I feel weak in my ability to rest.
3. Share your thoughts with your spouse.
4. While holding each other, ask your spouse to pray for you and invite Jesus to respond tenderly to those areas of need. Notice how this feels in your body and thoughts.
5. Look ahead to the exercise for *Day Sixteen* and think about what fun activity you can create.

**Bonus 1:**

- Take turns sharing what you appreciate about your spouse, especially as it relates to his/her weaknesses and strengths.

**Bonus 2:**

- Let your face light up and kiss your spouse like you did the first months of your marriage.

**Bonus 3:**

- Discuss references in Scripture where God responds tenderly to weakness.

## Chris and Jen Thoughts:

*While it is humbling to acknowledge and discuss areas of weakness and vulnerability, it is also joy-producing because you end up feeling closer to your spouse - as long as your spouse responds tenderly, kindly and warmly to what you share. I, Chris, found this exercise meaningful in that Jen and I do not need to pretend in our marriage; we desire to acknowledge problem-areas and look to each other for prayer and encouragement. This sort of interaction is a good model for how we can interact with Jesus and look to Him for His presence in our lives and in our brokenness.*

## Additional Resources:

- *Joy Starts Here* book at www.joystartshere.com
- *Jesus In Mind* Talks, Volume 7, 16 and 29 at www.joystartshere.com
- Connexus for a thriving community at www.joystartshere.com
- *The Complete Guide to Living with Men* by E. James Wilder at www.joystartshere.com
- *THRIVE Training* at www.thrivetoday.org
    - *Reach Your Potential with Joy* Maturity Retreats
    - *Joy Rekindled* Marriage Retreats
    - Training Tracks I, II and III
    - THRIVE 52-week Skill Guides

## *DAY 15 NOTES - THOUGHTS - OBSERVATIONS:*

# Day Sixteen

## Play

Play is any activity that is free from purpose yet structured enough to feel safe and have fun without serious consequences. Evidence indicates that the greatest rewards of play come when it arises naturally from within.[1] Play promotes brain growth. Play creates new neural connections in the brain and tests them. Play lets us bond and build joy together. Simply, play is FUN!

Studies show play in the form of puzzles, playful exercise, games and other forms of play lead to resistance to neurodegenerative diseases (Alzheimer's, dementia, MS, etc.).[2] The amount of play we have is correlated to the development of the brain's frontal cortex. The frontal cortex is the region that discriminates relevant from irrelevant information, monitors and organizes our own thoughts and feelings and plans for the future.[3] At THRIVE we know a key part of this area as Level 4 of the control center.

---

1. Stuart Brown, M.D. Play. Page 104.

2. Page 59.

3. Page 34.

## Your Brain's Novelty Detector

Studies show people grow closer when they try something new together. Doing something new helps you build memories that last and strengthens long-term memories. Novelty promotes better memory, and we want to use this research for our next exercise. (*See additional information for more on this science*).

## Bonding With Fun And Play

With this in mind we are going to practice engaging your brain's novelty detector for a bit of play. This exercise requires some foresight, so plan accordingly.

1. Warm up your relational circuits.
2. Find a new activity to do that is interactive, engaging and fun. (Go fly a kite, play hacky sack, swing at a playground, thumb-wrestle, throw a Frisbee, give piggy back rides, ride your bicycles, play charades, play cards or a board game, etc.) *The more creative and interactive the exercise, the better this will be for you.*
3. Discuss with your spouse what was satisfying or not about your play time.
4. After this fun activity, do you feel like your attachment light is now on with your spouse?
    a. **Light on:** I want to connect. I desire your presence. I feel motivated to have your attention. I want your affection.
    b. **Light off:** I want to be alone. I want to rest. I want to do my own thing without interruptions. I don't want to interact with you right now. I want to play with my phone, computer or engage in non-relational activities.

**Bonus 1:**

- Discuss practical ways you can easily insert play into your week.

**Bonus 2:**

- Let your face light up and kiss your spouse like you did the first months of your marriage.

## Additional Information:

Your brain's hippocampus is one of the most important brain regions involved in processing and storing memories along with sensory impressions. New stimuli activates this region of the brain more than familiar stimuli. The hippocampus compares incoming sensory information with stored experience and knowledge. When there is a contrast of information, the hippocampus sends dopamine to another part of the brain called substantia nigra (SN) and the ventral tegmental area (*VTA – part of the brain's reward system*) in the midbrain. From there, nerve fibers extend back to the hippocampus and trigger the release of more dopamine.

Dopamine is a motivating neurotransmitter that is key to your brain's reward system. This feedback loop is why we remember things better in the context of novelty. A 2003 study led by researcher Shaomin Li and colleagues at Trinity College in Dublin found the release of dopamine in the hippocampus of rats activates the synapses among nerve cells, thus creating stronger connections that lead to long term memory storage.[4] Something new means *pay attention!*

4. Learning by Surprise by Daniela Fenker and Hartmut Schutze, Dec. 2008/Jan. 2009 Scientific American Mind, Page 47.

## Chris and Jen Thoughts:

*Play is something I (Jen) struggle with. I tend to be a planner, usually to a rigid degree. It feels like a lot of work for me to "be flexible" which means playfulness does not come naturally. Thankfully, God gave me a husband who enjoys "play" and likes to have fun. Practicing play has been good for our marriage and healthy for my relationship with my sons. I want my boys to grow up with a Mommy who is playful and fun, not just efficient.*

*For this exercise Jen and I (Chris) went to a park to fly kites. There is simply nothing like flying a kite and I found myself having fun, smiling, laughing and enjoying Jen and the boys. Not only did we build meaningful memories but we bonded together as a family. We enjoyed ourselves. It made me feel closer to my family.*

## Additional Resources:

- *THRIVE-at-Home* online program at www.thrivetoday.org
- *Jesus In Mind* Talks, Volume 13, 15 and 17 at www.joystartshere.com
- Connexus for a thriving community at www.joystartshere.com
- T*HRIVE Training* at www.thrivetoday.org
    - o *Reach Your Potential with Joy* Maturity Retreats
    - o *Joy Rekindled* Marriage Retreats
    - o Training Tracks I, II and III
    - o THRIVE 52-week Skill Guides

## *DAY 16 NOTES - THOUGHTS - OBSERVATIONS:*

# Day Seventeen

The bonus about interacting with Immanuel is He knows just what we need in order to have peace and shalom when something troubles us. Often He is the only One who can give us the perspective, thought, comfort, image, etc. that introduces the peace we have been searching for. One of the main reasons we have you start your Immanuel practice from a place of appreciation is because *this is the most likely brain state* for you to be able to perceive a clear awareness of God's presence. It is not like God suddenly shows up once you practice appreciation; rather, you *reach the optimum state* for your body and nervous system to recognize God's active presence.

From a place of appreciation (and interaction with God) you can find out what He wants you to know about what is bothering you. Most of us have habits that irritate, bother or frustrate us. The wonderful thing in all of this is that Jesus has something He wants you to know that will increase your peace, even if the behavior or habit never changes! Instead of focusing on our spouse, we will shine the light on ourselves.

If you do not find peace in this brief time of Immanuel interaction, do not give up. Spend some additional time in prayer (with a friend if necessary) until you find His shalom-peace that helps you breathe more easily. Read the Immanuel overview on page 189 for more details.

## Immanuel Intervention For Irritations

1. Warm up your relational circuits.
2. Individually, reflect on an appreciation or interactive memory with Jesus.
3. Individually, talk with Immanuel about one behavior/quality/habit you have that is an irritant, bother or nuisance for you. (Examples: I bite my fingernails, I go to bed too late, I forget to turn off room lights in the house, I watch too much television, I do not exercise enough, etc.)
4. Ask Immanuel if there is anything He wants you to know about this today. If you lose your peace or Immanuel awareness, return to your appreciation memory to interact with Him.
5. After spending a few minutes individually with Immanuel, find your spouse for the next steps.
6. If you felt Jesus shared a thought or picture with you that brought shalom-peace, share this with your spouse. If you do not have shalom-peace, share with your partner some qualities you appreciate about him/her. (Continue your dialogue with Immanuel until you have shalom-peace, and if necessary, have someone pray with you. You can then share with your spouse once you have clarity.)
7. While doing heart to heart holding, pray that Immanuel will give you patience and understanding for yourself and your spouse as well as restore areas and places that need healing and peace. Invite your spouse to join you in talking with Immanuel about the things about yourself that bother you. Ask Jesus for help to see yourself and Your spouse through His eyes.

**Bonus 1:**

- Practice one of the joy smile exercises with or without music (page 9).

**Bonus 2:**

- Discuss what you have been noticing about your relational circuits. Are patterns emerging where your relational circuits are on more than other times?

## Additional Information:

Shalom-peace is the transition from something that bothers you and internally feels unsettling to a calmer, quiet, serene impression that says, "I am not alone. I will be taken care of." Something may still be disturbing or circumstances may still be difficult, but the addition of shalom-peace means I now feel at ease in my own shoes, even in the middle of it all. An example would be a child who fears an upcoming dental cleaning and wants to scream, run and hide. With the help of an available, soothing parent who validates and comforts the child, he may still feel resistance to the procedure but he no longer feels alone because daddy is nearby holding his hands and looking on. Shalom-peace is the addition of rest and calm to a feeling or situation that feels unsettling or distressing.

Throughout Scripture we see the results of shalom-peace. Consider the feelings King David shares in Psalm 23: "Even though I walk through the valley of the shadow of death, I will fear no evil, for you are with me; your rod and staff, they comfort me. You prepare a table before me in the presence of my enemies…" (NIV) Shalom-peace helps David in the middle of difficulty. Then we have the scenario of Shadrach, Meshach and Abednego who, faced with death by a decree from King Nebuchadnezzar for their unwillingness to bend the knee to his gold statue, respond with: "King Nebuchadnezzar, we do not need to defend ourselves before you in this matter. If we are thrown into the blazing furnace, the God we serve is able to deliver us from it, and he will deliver us from Your Majesty's hand. But even if he does not, we want you to know, Your Majesty, that we will not serve your gods or worship the image of gold you have set up" Daniel 3:16b-18, (NIV). The three men were faced with incredible odds yet they remember who they are in the middle of it. At one point in His ministry, Jesus calms raging, stormy waters so the disciples could experience shalom-peace (Matthew 8, Mark 4). The addition of shalom-peace to unsettled feelings is that I can now breathe and feel a warm, soothing calm in my body and my thoughts.

### Chris and Jen Thoughts:

*I (Chris) tend to be hard on myself, so I find it life-giving when I interact with Immanuel and receive His patience, validation and comfort that brings me new-found hope and encouragement. Each of us is a work in progress, and this exercise can provide some much needed joy and even a bit of heart healing. May God bless you in this!*

## Additional Resources:

- *Joyful Journey* book at www.joystartshere.com
- *Share Immanuel* booklet at www.lifemodel.org
- *Jesus In Mind* Talks, Volumes 12, 13 and 20 at www.joystartshere.com
- *THRIVE Training* at www.thrivetoday.org
    - o *Joy Rekindled* Marriage Retreats
    - o Training Tracks I, II and III
    - o THRIVE 52-week Skill Guides
- *Joy Starts Here* at joystartshere.com
- *Outsmarting Yourself* by Dr. Karl and Charlotte Lehman
    - o www.kclehman.com, www.outsmartingyourself.org, www.immanuelapproach.com

## DAY 17 NOTES - THOUGHTS - OBSERVATIONS:

# Day Eighteen

We want to keep our joy levels high, and this exercise gives you some practice showing and sharing your joy. Anytime you "tell" a nonverbal story you are giving your brain's control center a solid workout. You will discover that using your face and body is fun and also very meaningful. Have fun and if you have time, try this exercise two or three times. Jump in the water - it feels great!

## Show And Share Your Joy

1. Warm up your relational circuits.
2. First person tell a nonverbal story about a shared joy memory. Be creative and see if your spouse can figure out what story you are telling.
3. Second person tell the story back to your spouse and add words and narrative to the nonverbal elements. This means you still "act" out the story to your partner but fill in the story with words, descriptions and sensations. (The plan is that you are able to figure out what story your partner has shared.)

4. Take turns so that each of you tell your nonverbal stories.
5. Discuss this exercise while doing heart to heart holding.
6. Thank Jesus for your partner out loud, so your partner can hear.
7. Look ahead to tomorrow's exercise for *Day Nineteen*, as it needs to be practiced during a meal.

**Bonus 1:**

- If you have time, try the exercise again with a new story.

**Bonus 2:**

- Discuss ways that your parents and family members dealt with conflict. How would you like to be different or improve on these examples? How can you increase joy while decreasing time spent in negative emotions and conflict?

## Additional Information:

Nonverbal stories are similar to charades where you can use your face, body, movements, gestures and voice tone to convey your thoughts. The more animated and creative you are, the better!

## Chris and Jen Thoughts:

*Jen and I practiced this exercise while we were very tired and preparing for bed. We noticed an immediate response of smiles and laughter while attempting the exercise. While some aspects of our stories were difficult to figure out, we interpreted most of the story elements so we could tell our stories back. It was fun!*

## Additional Resources:

- *Jesus In Mind* Talks, Volume 3, 5 and 23 at www.joystartshere.com
- Connexus for a thriving community at www.joystartshere.com
- *THRIVE Training* at www.thrivetoday.org
    - *Joy Rekindled* Marriage Retreats
    - Training Tracks I, II and III
    - THRIVE 52-week Skill Guides
- *Joy Starts Here* at joystartshere.com
- *The Complete Guide to Living with Men* by E. James Wilder at www.joystartshere.com
- *Outsmarting Yourself* by Dr. Karl and Charlotte Lehman
    - www.kclehman.com, www.outsmartingyourself.org, www.immanuelapproach.com

## *DAY 18 NOTES - THOUGHTS - OBSERVATIONS:*

# Day Nineteen

Mealtimes are one of the ideal times to bond and grow joy. We want to use this opportunity to have everyone at the table shift into a relational mode and be prepared for meaningful connections. Many couples miss this ideal window to sit down and eat together and start joy. Here is your chance to make the most of your family meals, even if family mealtime does not happen daily in your house. This exercise requires a bit of foresight so plan accordingly.

## Food, Bonding And Blessing

1. For the remaining fifteen minutes *before* dinner is served, while the cook is putting final touches on the meal, have the spouse who is not cooking do a fun, playful activity with the kids to let them burn off some energy and help their relational circuits warm up. (For couples without children at home, focus on helping the cook however he or she needs help such as setting the table, doing dishes, etc. While helping the cook, offer to tell joy

stories while he or she prepares the meal, assuming the stories are not distracting).

2. Sing the dinner prayer that you learned earlier while your face lights up. (*Demonstration is on YouTube at the* ***Chris Coursey - THRIVE*** *channel*).
3. At the beginning of dinner, family members express qualities you appreciate about the cook.
4. Discuss creative ways you can bring each other more joy.
5. Try to "get" as many joy smiles as possible out of the other family members at the table. Let your face light up, have fun interacting but respect overwhelm levels so that rest is part of the fun.
6. Near the end of the meal, take time for everyone to thank Jesus for food and family.

**Bonus:**

- Everyone help clear the table and clean the kitchen while the cook rests and watches.

## Chris and Jen Thoughts:

*With young children (1 and 3) who frequently melt down by dinner time, this exercise is especially wonderful when Chris is able to do it. I feel that it helps me stay grounded during the final moments of dinner preparation. It helps the boys come to the table in a better mood so we have the best possible chance to be in relational mode instead of overwhelm mode, which enables us to start joy and bond as we eat.*

## Additional Resources:

- *Jesus In Mind* Talks, Volume 8, 13 and 28 at www.joystartshere.com
- *Joy Starts Here* at joystartshere.com
- *The Complete Guide to Living with Men* by E. James Wilder at www.joystartshere.com

## *DAY 19 NOTES - THOUGHTS - OBSERVATIONS:*

# Day Twenty

Skill Eleven of the Nineteen Skills (Appendix B) is our ability to return to joy from negative emotions. The lack of this skill can have a negative effect on our marriages. With relational skills dropping out of families and communities at an alarming rate, it is rare to find a couple who can return to joy from all six negative emotions. When we do not return to joy from any of the "big six" emotions we are wired for, we side-track from one emotion to another or we stay stuck in the emotion. We may even avoid particular emotions without realizing it. Examples would be people-pleasing to avoid shame or working hard to avoid anger because anger scares us.

Our marriages are strengthened and preserved when we identify areas where Skill Eleven is weak. We learn to return to joy from a negative emotion because someone with the skill - a "trained brain" shows us how it works. If there is an area you are weak, this exercise is your opportunity to bring this weakness to Jesus and discover what He wants you to know. Jesus can lead you to learn Skill Eleven and help you find resources.

# Introduction To Skill Eleven: *Return To Joy*

1. Warm up your relational circuits.
2. Discuss what emotions you prefer. What emotions do you avoid?
    a. Anger
    b. Sadness
    c. Fear
    d. Shame
    e. Disgust
    f. Hopeless Despair
3. Discuss how you respond when your spouse becomes stuck longer than 90 seconds in a negative emotion? (Example: *When you feel hopeless I feel powerless so I become angry to make it stop.*)
4. What are some of the reasons that best explain your intensified reactions? (Example: *I feel like I have to fix you when you are stuck and this reminds me of the time…*)
5. Take a moment to remember an interactive or appreciation memory.
6. Ask Jesus what He wants you to know about your strengths and weaknesses as it relates to the six negative emotions. Share any thoughts that come to mind.
7. Take some time to pray for the emotional vulnerabilities in each other and how these impact your marriage joy.

**Bonus 1:**

- Tell a joy story then take three minutes of heart to heart quieting.

**Bonus 2:**

- Tell short stories about times you experienced a negative emotion and someone helped you return to joy. Avoid stories of personal loss and practice your four-plus story telling skills from the worksheet on page 72.

**Bonus 3:**

- Discuss the strengths and weaknesses of your parents when it comes to returning to joy from the big six emotions.

## Chris and Jen Thoughts:

*When I, Jen, was first introduced to the six emotions, sadness was the only emotion from which I could moderately return to joy. Sadness tends to be one of the more manageable emotions from the list that most people can do. As Chris and I identified our weaknesses with Skill Eleven, our relationship began to make more sense, particularly when one of us encountered a certain emotion. We found people who use Skill Eleven, and they graciously helped us learn the skill which we now use in our marriage and family. Skill Eleven has made a dramatic difference in our marriage and other relationships as well. Hopeless despair and shame tend to be more difficult emotions, so if you do not already have Skill Eleven, start with an easier emotion then work up to the harder ones.*

*When I did Step 6 of this exercise and interacted with Jesus, I was pleasantly surprised by the thought and image that He was rejoicing with me over how far I have come in my growth with Skill Eleven. I felt like He wanted me to spend some time with Him appreciating and celebrating where I was before and where I am now. This was very encouraging to us!*

## Additional Resources:

- *Jesus In Mind* Talks, Volume 3, 9, 12, 14, 16 and 29 at www.joystartshere.com
- *Share Immanuel* booklet at www.joystartshere.com
- *The Complete Guide to Living with Men* by E. James Wilder at www.joystartshere.com
- Connexus for a thriving community at www.joystartshere.com
- *THRIVE Training* at www.thrivetoday.org
    - *Joy Rekindled* Marriage Retreats
    - Training Tracks I, II and III
    - THRIVE 52-week Skill Guides
- *Joy Starts Here* at joystartshere.com
- *Outsmarting Yourself* by Dr. Karl and Charlotte Lehman
    - www.kclehman.com, www.outsmartingyourself.org, www.immanuelapproach.com

## *DAY 20 NOTES - THOUGHTS - OBSERVATIONS:*

# Day Twenty-One

The goal of this exercise is to experience appreciation moments with your spouse. Appreciation can be enjoyed with a partner, by yourself or with Jesus. Appreciation warms up your relational circuits. This exercise is especially fun to do with your spouse because hearing what your spouse appreciates about you and getting to share what you appreciate about him or her brings a secure feeling and deepens your bond. We end up feeling respected, valued and loved when we express appreciation to our beloved! (*This exercise is Taken from the Year One Mastering Joy and Quiet Basic Skill Guide.*)

## Three, Three And Three Appreciation

1. Warm up your relational circuits.
2. Preferably at the end of a day, express to your spouse three things you appreciate from your day. Use specific examples and describe what each moment felt like in your body. (An example would be, "I enjoyed seeing my nephew today. When his face lit up and he ran toward me, I felt warm and excited...")

3. When you finish, let your spouse do the same.
4. Next, express three qualities you appreciate about God; use specific examples and express how it feels as you think about these qualities. (An example would be, "I appreciate God's patience with me because I often push myself hard and sometimes forget to have my quiet time, but God waits patiently for me to talk with Him. I feel hopeful and calm when I think of God patiently waiting for me," etc.)
5. When you finish, let your spouse do the same.
6. Last, express three things you appreciate about your spouse. Use examples and share how you feel as you reflect on these qualities. (An example would be, "I appreciate the fact that you were glad to be with me when I returned home from the grocery store. Your joy encouraged me and I felt safe and joyful...")
7. Let your spouse do the same.
8. Discuss how you feel after doing this exercise. What do you notice?

**Bonus 1:**

- Practice heart to heart holding and rest.

**Bonus 2:**

- Take a moment and invite Immanuel to show you what He was doing during this exercise. Share the thoughts that come to mind.

## Chris and Jen Thoughts:

*By far this is one of my (Jen) favorite exercises. Chris and I created this exercise because I was having trouble sleeping at night. I would sometimes toss and turn for hours, unable to quiet my mind and go to sleep. We found that after about 15 minutes of going through this exercise together, we both felt a warm, peaceful feeling and could usually fall asleep in just a few moments. My favorite part is hearing what Chris appreciates about me as this always leaves me with a warm, fuzzy, secure feeling. I am excited for you to try this!*

*Jen and I (Chris) practiced this exercise late one night after a long day so we started out feeling low energy and physically tired. The results of appreciation were noticeable quickly as we started to smile, relax and enjoy each other's presence. It was a fun exercise and no matter how many times we practice this exercise we continue to enjoy it every time.*

## Additional Resources:

- *Joy Starts Here* at joystartshere.com
- *THRIVE Training* at www.thrivetoday.org
    - o *Joy Rekindled* Marriage Retreats
    - o Training Tracks I, II and III
    - o THRIVE 52-week Skill Guides
    - o THRIVE-at-Home online training at www.thrivetoday.org
- Connexus for a thriving community at www.joystartshere.com
- *Jesus In Mind* Talks, Volume 3 and 7 at www.joystartshere.com
- *The Complete Guide to Living with Men* by E. James Wilder at www.joystartshere.com
- *Outsmarting Yourself* by Dr. Karl and Charlotte Lehman
    - o www.kclehman.com, www.outsmartingyourself.org, www.immanuelapproach.com

## *DAY 21 NOTES - THOUGHTS - OBSERVATIONS:*

# Day Twenty-Two

## Relational Sandwiches

Relational sandwiches are a practical exercise designed to prevent problems from becoming bigger than relationships. Psalmists and prophets frequently "make sandwiches" to express grievances, prayers and praise. This structure is a natural part of Hebrew thought and poetry. We use the visual metaphor of a sandwich to describe how we start with the relationship, put the problem in the middle, then end with the relationship.

This description with all the example exercises are used with permission from *Joy Starts Here - The Transformation Zone* by E. James Wilder, Edward M. Khouri, Chris M. Coursey and Shelia D. Sutton (2013). Available at www.joystartshere.com.

**The flow looks like this:**

1. Importance of relationship (historic)
2. Current event (problem)
3. Importance of relationship (relational outcome)

The third part of this sandwich is not how you want the problem resolved; rather, it is what kind of relationship you want as a result.

**Personal Example:**
1. We have been friends for a long time and I like being with you.
2. But when you cut me off when I am speaking I feel like you are not listening.
3. I want us to have a relationship where we really understand each other. (Notice that we have focused on the kind of relationship we want instead of how we want the problem resolved.)

**Psalm 51 Example (NKJV):**
1. "Have mercy upon me, O God, according to Your lovingkindness; according to the multitude of Your tender mercies, blot out my transgressions" (Verse 1).
2. "For I acknowledge my transgressions, and my sin is always before me" (Verse 3).
3. "Restore to me the joy of Your salvation, and uphold me by Your generous Spirit" (Verse 12).

## Sandwich Making

1. Warm up your relational circuits.
2. As a couple practice building a relational sandwich together with God about any active concerns, fears or pressing needs that you both have regarding money, health, work or strained relationships.
3. Take turns so that each of you practice this individually (out loud) with God for your own concerns as well as together for your shared concerns. Do this as many times as you desire for issues that are bothering you.
4. Discuss what you notice after practicing this exercise.

**Bonus 1:**

- Take turns telling stories about times you feel like God answered a prayer and provided for you in the midst of a difficult situation.

**Bonus 2:**

- Practice joy smiles then close by praying for God's face to shine on your spouse and marriage.

**Bonus 3:**

- If you are really ambitious, try this exercise again, but focus on your spouse. The goal is to practice the relational sandwich with a minor irritant rather than *the big issue we have never been able to resolve that overwhelms us to think about.* Begin with the importance of your relationship which reminds you the problem is minor in comparison to the value of your relationship. Share your concern then finish with how you want to see the relationship after your interaction. (*We credit Jim Wilder and the Joy Starts Here book for relational sandwich training.*)

1. Warm up your relational circuits.
2. As a couple practice building a relational sandwich for minor irritants such as your spouse failed to put dishes away, sprayed water on the bathroom counter and forgot to clean it up or left a light on in the house.
3. Take turns so that each of you can practice this for your own situations.
4. Discuss what you notice after practicing this exercise.
5. Pray and thank God for your spouse.

## Chris and Jen Thoughts:

*Chris – Day 22 proved to be special for Jen and I for a number of reasons. My day was particularly painful regarding a relational strain and I was all too eager to talk with Immanuel about my burden. Doing the relational sandwich brought much needed perspective, peace and comfort. While I was already feeling relief and clarity, Bonus 1 was wonderful because Jen and I reminisced for a time about the amazing ways God has answered prayer and proven Himself faithful over and over again.*

*My day went from difficult and painful to refreshing and peaceful. Not a bad ending to the day!*

## Additional Resources:

- *Joy Starts Here* at joystartshere.com
- *Jesus In Mind* Talks, Volume 26 at www.joystartshere.com

## *DAY 22 NOTES - THOUGHTS - OBSERVATIONS:*

# Day Twenty-Three

*Day Twenty-Three* is an insightful exercise because it allows you and your spouse to consider the impact of your words and emotions for joy or for pain. You have the opportunity to see that your spouse recognizes the impact he or she had on you when a response was not tender. It is meaningful to hear how the other person would have preferred to respond which helps us see the person behind the malfunction. We suggest you be creative and animated for this exercise and try to clearly convey your thoughts and impressions.

## **Tender Responses:** *Missing In Action*

1. Warm up your relational circuits.
2. One of you tell a nonverbal story about a moment *you failed to respond tenderly* to your spouse.
    a. As part of your story, demonstrate the effect your reaction had on him or her.
3. When you finish, tell your story with words then include how

you would have wanted to respond if you could press the reset button and do it all over again.

4. Next, nonverbally convey a quality you appreciate about your spouse. Then use words to share this quality.
5. Switch roles.
6. Discuss the exercise.
7. Look ahead to the exercise for *Day Twenty-Four* in case you need any prep for the fun that happens tomorrow.

**Bonus 1:**

- Invite Immanuel to share how He responds tenderly to your weaknesses. Share any possible Immanuel thoughts with your spouse.

**Bonus 2:**

- Practice heart to heart holding as you quiet and rest.

## Chris and Jen Thoughts:

*Jen and I enjoyed this exercise. What made the steps so meaningful for us was to acknowledge recent events where we both failed to respond tenderly toward the other. When we shared how we would have wanted to respond we found this refreshing and comforting.*

*During the Immanuel time I specifically felt Immanuel encourage me:*

- *Jesus responds to my weaknesses by inviting me to rest.*
- *Jesus gives me permission to take care of myself rather than "push harder."*
- *Jesus is not surprised by my weakness and, in fact, seems pleased when Jen and I bring our weaknesses to Him for validation, attunement and comfort.*

## Additional Resources:

- *Joy Starts Here* book at joystartshere.com
- *THRIVE Training* at www.thrivetoday.org
    - o *Joy Rekindled* Marriage Retreats
    - o Training Tracks I, II and III
    - o THRIVE 52-week Skill Guides
    - o THRIVE-at-Home online program at www.thrivetoday.org
- *Joyful Journey* book at www.joystartshere.com
- Connexus for a thriving community at www.joystartshere.com
- *Jesus In Mind* Talks, Volumes 11 and 29 at www.joystartshere.com
- *Share Immanuel* booklet at www.joystartshere.com

## *DAY 23 NOTES - THOUGHTS - OBSERVATIONS:*

# Day Twenty-Four

There was a time in human history when people used ink and paper as a method for communication. We want to revive this ancient custom, at least for this exercise, and have you practice appreciation the old fashion way. Write something meaningful on a card or paper, then share it with your mate. Be sincere, and by all means, even a bit romantic! This exercise requires a bit of forethought and preparation.

## Appreciation Card

1. Warm up your relational circuits.
2. Think (and ask Immanuel) about at least three ways your spouse blesses you.
3. Write a love note or card to your spouse. Include thoughts from the previous step.
4. Place the card somewhere your spouse will find it, such as a briefcase, on the coffee maker, on the bathroom mirror, etc.
5. When you come together, tell your spouse the things he/she says and does that make your face light up and make you feel special.

6. Notice and discuss how appreciation feels in your body as you express these glad to be together feelings with each other.
7. Let your face light up and kiss your spouse.

**Bonus:**

- Discuss relational circuit awareness: did this exercise move you into a more relational mode? What was fun about this exercise?

## Chris and Jen Thoughts:

*I feel loved and special when Chris writes me a card because I have something I can save in order to look at later and experience appreciation all over again! I still have most of the cards Chris has given me since we started dating, and I still enjoy looking back at them.*

*I Chris, have kept most of the cards Jen has given me as well, though she has given me more than I have given her so my dresser drawer runneth over. This exercise is fun because it gives us a chance to bless our spouse and use our words in a meaningful way. My only challenge for this exercise was to write my letter clearly because I have sloppy handwriting. For those of you who can relate, do your best to make your cards legible!*

## Additional Resources:

- *THRIVE Training* at www.thrivetoday.org
    - *Joy Rekindled* Marriage Retreats
    - Training Tracks I, II and III
    - THRIVE 52-week Skill Guides
    - THRIVE-at-Home online program at www.thrivetoday.org
- Connexus for a thriving community at www.joystartshere.com
- *Jesus In Mind* Talks, Volumes 3, 10, 12 and 13 at www.joystartshere.com
- *Joyful Journey* book at www.joystartshere.com
- *Share Immanuel* booklet at www.joystartshere.com
- *The Complete Guide to Living with Men* by E. James Wilder at www.joystartshere.com

## *DAY 24 NOTES - THOUGHTS - OBSERVATIONS:*

# Day Twenty-Five

One of the more meaningful exercises to practice for your marriage involves talking with Jesus about how and what He prays for *as it relates to your marriage and spouse.* Scripture provides refreshing insight into the reality that we have an Intercessor before the Father who prays and intercedes on our behalf. This Intercessor, Jesus Christ, knows our needs, our weaknesses, our struggles and our temptations. (*See Additional Information for a few of the Scripture passages that provide insight into this.*)

What is more special than joining Immanuel in prayer for your spouse? *Day Twenty-Five* gives you a meaningful introduction to this simple yet profound exercise.

## Pray Like Jesus Prays

1. Warm up your relational circuits.
2. Focus on one of your appreciation or interactive memories with Immanuel until you feel peaceful shalom in your mind and body.

3. As you remember your appreciation memory or begin to develop the awareness of Immanuel's presence with you, invite Immanuel to show you how He prays and intercedes for your partner. Notice what thoughts come to mind and continue to invite God to show you more as it relates to the following questions.
    a. "Lord, what do You enjoy about my marriage?"
    b. "What do You delight in as it relates to my spouse?
4. After some time of prayer, take turns praying for each other including the thoughts you feel may have been "Immanuel inspired."
5. Discuss this exercise.

**Bonus 1:**

- Take turns telling stories about times you feel like God answered a prayer during a difficult time in your marriage.

**Bonus 2:**

- Practice joy smiles then finish with heart to heart quieting. At the end, let your face light up and kiss your spouse like you did in the first months of your marriage.

**Bonus 3:**

- Try the exercise once again after the bonus steps to see what happens now that you may be in a more relational mode. Include how Jesus prays for the weaknesses in your spouse.

# Additional Information:

A few Scriptural references where Jesus intercedes for us:

- "Who is he that condemns? Christ Jesus, who died--more than that, who was raised to life --is at the right hand of God and is also interceding for us" Romans 8:34 (NIV).
- "Therefore he is able to save completely those who come to God through him, because he always lives to intercede for them" Hebrews 7:25 (NIV).

- "For we do not have a high priest who is unable to sympathize with our weaknesses, but we have one who has been tempted in every way, just as we are – yet was without sin. Let us then approach the throne of grace with confidence, so that we may receive mercy and find grace to help us in our time of need" Hebrews 4:15-16 (NIV).
- "My dear children, I write this to you so that you will not sin. But if anybody does sin, we have one who speaks to the Father in our defense – Jesus Christ, the Righteous One" 1 John 2:1 (NIV).

## Chris and Jen Thoughts:

*Even though I know Jen pretty well at this point in our marriage, I am frequently surprised by the thoughts that come to mind when we practice this exercise. Jesus can use existing information you already know about your spouse but it's fun to experience a new thought, image or something that feels like it was Immanuel inspired. Go on, be surprised and have fun with this one!*

## Additional Resources:

- *Joy Starts Here* book at www.joystartshere.com
- *Joyful Journey* book at www.joystartshere.com
- *Jesus In Mind* Talks, Volume 12, 21 and 26 at www.joystartshere.com
- *Share Immanuel* booklet at www.joystartshere.com

## *DAY 25 NOTES - THOUGHTS - OBSERVATIONS:*

# Day Twenty-Six

The goal of this exercise, *Generational Strengths and Weaknesses*, is to acknowledge the prevalence of generational patterns and notice where you have made changes and outgrown some unwanted patterns. Keep in mind that we are all a work in progress and the goal is not to "beat ourselves up" for the areas we still struggle. With that said, it is encouraging to see where we have developed our relational skill set beyond what our parents and previous generations learned and used. You *can* make a difference in your marriage as it relates to what was passed on to you and what you have earned. Have fun expressing some love to your spouse and highlighting the strengths you appreciate in him or her!

## Generational Strengths And Weaknesses

1. Warm up your relational circuits.
2. Look at the list on page 160 then identify some of your parents' strengths and weaknesses.
3. Discuss how these generational patterns impact your marriage.

4. Where have you developed greater strengths than your parents in the examples below under Additional Information?
5. Take turns telling nonverbal stories about three strengths that you observe and appreciate in your spouse. When finished, use words to share the strengths you appreciate.
6. While heart to heart holding, tell your spouse the qualities that made you fall in love with him or her.
7. Look ahead to the exercise for *Day Twenty-Seven* to be "on your game" for tomorrow.

**Bonus:**

- Discuss three qualities you appreciate as it relates to your mother and father. (Or other authority figures such as a grandparent, coach, teacher, etc.) Express these in a letter or face to face interaction. If they are no longer here, take a moment to thank God for these people.

## Additional Information:

**Identify relational strengths and weaknesses in both parents when it comes to:**

- Resolving conflicts
- Resting and quieting
- Staying relational (and returning to joy) when feeling:
    - Upset
    - Tired or hungry
    - Angry and the big six emotions
    - Overwhelmed
    - Hurt or offended
- Achieving mutual satisfaction
- Sharing weaknesses and vulnerabilities with each other
- Using mealtimes to bring joy
- Responding tenderly to weaknesses and malfunctions

## Chris and Jen Thoughts:

*Chris and I frequently notice that a number of the relational issues we struggle with are familiar patterns we learned growing up. These patterns were present for our parents and even previous generations. To varying degrees, these patterns spill into our marriage. While this does not give us an excuse to allow unwanted responses, we notice that we are more sympathetic and understanding toward our spouse when we remember this piece of history then practice "Godsight," or Skill Thirteen, to see each other as God sees him or her. As we recognize that the other person is responding from patterns learned in their family, we stay mindful that these patterns are easily learned and often difficult to sever. As we keep our relational circuits on we can offer tender responses that are satisfying and helpful so that true change occurs.*

*It was meaningful for me, Chris, to discuss the areas I have grown because, let's face it, when hiking in the mountains it is all too easy to see how much ground you still need to cover and then feel discouraged. However, when you take a moment to review how much ground you already covered, it can feel very encouraging and uplifting. Jen and I had a lot of fun with this exercise, especially the nonverbal stories. After a long day this exercise resettled our nervous systems and we went to bed peacefully.*

## Additional Resources:

- *Joy Starts Here* at www.joystartshere.com
- *The Complete Guide to Living with Men* by E. James Wilder at www.joystartshere.com
- *THRIVE Training* at www.thrivetoday.org
    - *Joy Rekindled* Marriage Retreats
    - Training Tracks I, II and III
    - THRIVE 52-week Skill Guides
    - THRIVE-at-Home online program at www.thrivetoday.org
- Connexus for a thriving community at www.joystartshere.com
- *Jesus In Mind* Talks, Volume 11, 25, 26, 27 and 29 at www.joystartshere.com
- *Outsmarting Yourself* by Dr. Karl and Charlotte Lehman
    - www.kclehman.com, www.outsmartingyourself.org, www.immanuelapproach.com

## *DAY 26 NOTES - THOUGHTS - OBSERVATIONS:*

# Day Twenty-Seven

One of the blessings of being married involves the golden opportunity to serve your spouse. We serve because *we want* to bless our spouse, and serve God in joy as Ephesians 6:7 reminds us, "Serve wholeheartedly, as if you were serving the Lord, not men" (NIV). Serving free from obligation feels extra special and satisfying especially when we know something we have said or done makes our spouse feel cherished. Here is your opportunity to do something for your spouse that you know is meaningful and will make his or her face light up.

## Love That Serves

1. Warm up your relational circuits.
2. Do a small act of service for your spouse that you know will be meaningful. For example, you can complete an unfinished project around the house, wash his or her feet, clean the house, cook a meal, wash the dishes, clean the car, etc. Be creative and give this some creative thought and planning. Include a note express-

ing what you did and why you wanted to bless your spouse in this particular way.

3. When you come together, share with your spouse the most meaningful ways he or she serves you. Express your appreciation.
4. Notice if your attachment light comes on in response to giving or receiving the act of service as well as when you share appreciation. (*See Additional Information below for review.*)
5. Discuss possible signs that indicate your spouse's attachment light was on or off. Check these conclusions with your spouse.
6. Practice heart to heart holding.

**Bonus:**

- Tell a nonverbal story showing how you feel when your spouse does something thoughtful and considerate for you.
- When you finish, use words to fill in the blanks then discuss special moments where your spouse made you feel special.

## Additional Information:

If you remember from pages 64-66 about attachment lights and styles, you will notice your attachment light is on when you feel the inside "tug" and desire to interact with your spouse or have his or her attention and, along with your relational circuits, you feel a desire to talk, laugh, connect and enjoy meaningful interaction together. With a joyful response you feel peaceful, valued and seen.

If your attachment light is off you may prefer to be alone, "veg" or seek nonrelational activities and tasks instead of interaction with your spouse. It is worth noting that when your attachment light is "on" and your spouse does not respond, this becomes painful or frustrating, so we want to synchronize attachment lights which means interacting together then resting together, interacting then resting, and so forth.

## Chris and Jen Thoughts:

*What made this exercise fun for me (Chris) was how Jen initiated the exercise by cleaning the house. At this stage of life we both try to clean the house together, but life has been so full and busy that house cleaning tends to be low on our to-do list mostly because of limited time. To be honest, I actually forgot about the exercise until I found a sweet appreciation note on my desk from Jen after she cleaned the house while I was out. It was touching and made me smile.*

*For my part, I watered Jen's newly planted flowers in the backyard for a time since they were looking a bit "parched" on this hot day. I then left Jen a sweet note.*

*The exercise made both of us feel loved and special. I hope you enjoy this exercise!*

## Additional Resources:

- *Joy Starts Here* at www.joystartshere.com
- *THRIVE 52-week Skill Guides* at www.thrivetoday.org
- Connexus for a thriving community at www.joystartshere.com
- *Jesus In Mind* Talks, Volumes 13 and 20 at www.joystartshere.com

# *DAY 27 NOTES - THOUGHTS - OBSERVATIONS:*

# Day Twenty-Eight

As promised, you will see a number of exercises involving food. The goal with food is to make the most out of bonding over mealtimes by using joy as our catalyst. God designed fellowship meals as the ideal way to enhance relationships. God created a wonderful variety of colors, textures and flavors in foods to delight our palettes. God has given us each other to amplify joy and the good things we share with one another. Be sure to turn off the television and minimize distractions for this exercise.

## Food And Joy

1. During a meal with your spouse take turns telling stories about your favorite food memories growing up. Include the people and relationships that were a part of that time and why those moments were so special. The spouse with the strongest joy memories of these moments should go first.
2. List some of your favorite food memories with your spouse then share your stories including what makes your memories special.

3. Notice how you both feel as you remember and share these fond memories.
4. Discuss creative, simple ways you can continue to make mealtimes more joyful.
5. Share what you enjoyed about your meal - both the food and the interaction.

**Bonus 1:**

- Discuss at least three of your favorite joy moments from your day.

**Bonus 2:**

- Discuss what you are noticing about your relational circuits. Are patterns emerging?

**Favorite Food Memories:**

## Chris and Jen Thoughts:

*I, Jen, do not have a lot of joyful food memories that immediately come to mind when I think of my childhood. Chris started by sharing his joyful food memories first because he has a lot of special memories that made it easy for him to go first. As he was sharing, I began to remember some fun food memories from my past. This exercise turned out to be meaningful for both of us. We now hope to make more special food memories for us and our sons.*

## Additional Resources:

- *Joy Starts Here* at www.joystartshere.com
- *Jesus In Mind* Talks, Volume 15 and 28 at www.joystartshere.com
- Connexus for a thriving community at www.joystartshere.com
- *THRIVE 52-week Skill Guides* at www.thrivetoday.org
- *The Complete Guide to Living with Men* by E. James Wilder at www.joystartshere.com

## *DAY 28 NOTES - THOUGHTS - OBSERVATIONS:*

# Day Twenty-Nine

The promised exercise is here. God has brilliantly designed us to be relational creatures blessed with the opportunity for sexual union as an intimate expression of joy with our spouse. God created sexual union to be not only procreative but also a pleasurable and intense enhancer to bond with our spouse. Thanks to a plethora of chemicals, including oxytocin and dopamine, we both bond and experience an intense reward during intimacy with our mate.

Starting with our relational circuits warmed, we will cycle between high-energy activities that are arousing and low-energy activities that are calming. Alternating these two energy states can make for an intensely intimate and joyful sexual experience. We understand that trying to bring these directions to bed with you may feel a bit awkward and unromantic, but be a sport and give it a try! (*We thank Dr. Jim Wilder for the inspiration for this exercise as it is based on the sexuality exercise he created from the Joy Rekindled Marriage Retreat.*)

## Sexuality Exercise

1. Warm up your relational circuits.
2. While heart-to-heart holding, share three qualities you appreciate about your spouse's character. Be specific about times you have seen these qualities in action, preferably connected to joy memories.
3. Using playful but gentle sexual touch, try to get your partner's attachment light to turn on. **Note:** To avoid overwhelming your spouse, take moments of quiet and pause as needed.
4. Next, take a few moments for simple quiet together. As you quiet, you have two options.
    a. Put your hand on your spouse's chest so that you both can feel each other's heartbeat and synchronize breathing.
    b. Take turns listening to each other's heartbeat by putting your ear to your spouse's chest and synchronize breathing.

3. Share three qualities you appreciate and enjoy about your partner's body using words and light touch.
4. Make love.
5. While heart to heart holding, take turns thanking Jesus for your spouse loud enough so that your partner can hear you pray.

**Bonus:**

- Discuss what was satisfying about synchronizing attachments lights through sexuality. Did you feel attuned as a team in a mutually satisfying way?

## Chris and Jen Thoughts:

*I, Jen, like that this exercise is simple but the few extra steps add intimacy to the experience.*

*I, Chris, found this exercise restful and joyful in that there are steps to interact with your spouse that are gentle, intimate and comforting. Rather than simply "jumping into the water" of intimacy you have gradual relational steps to enjoy each other.*

*We pray you find this exercise meaningful for your bond.*

## Additional Resources:

- *Jesus In Mind* Talks, Volume 10 at www.joystartshere.com
- *THRIVE 52-week Skill Guides* at www.thrivetoday.org
- *The Complete Guide to Living with Men* by E. James Wilder at www.joystartshere.com
- *THRIVE Training* at www.thrivetoday.org
    - *Joy Rekindled* Marriage Retreats

## *DAY 29 NOTES - THOUGHTS - OBSERVATIONS:*

# Day Thirty

Your final exercise has arrived: CONGRATULATIONS!

If you made it this far in your thirty days of joy exercises, you have covered some serious ground. *Day Thirty* is all about reviewing your journey and appreciating the highs while learning and regrouping from the lows.

## Looking Back *but* Moving Forward

1. Warm up your relational circuits.
2. Discuss what you feel you learned from the exercises in the *Thirty Days of JOY* handbook.
3. What have you noticed about your relational circuits?
4. Tell your spouse the qualities you discovered that you appreciate about him or her during this "joy journey."
5. What three things can you do in your marriage to increase joy? Your ideas should be simple and practical.
6. Practice joy smiles with or without music.

7. When finished, kiss your spouse like you did in the early months of your marriage.
8. Close with heart to heart holding.

**Bonus 1:**

- Repeat the *Day Twenty-Nine* exercise.

**Bonus 2:**

- Repeat your favorite exercise from the handbook.

**Bonus 3:**

- Finish your journey of joy by measuring your joy levels to compare the results of your joy growth. Visit www.joyq.joystartshere.com to take your free assessment. Compare notes with your spouse.

**Bonus 4:**

- Continue to increase your joy growth with the following next steps. You can join or lead a *Joy Starts Here* small group study, practice joy as a community with the Connexus curriculum or attend a *THRIVE Training* to boost your joy and practice the nineteen skills. Visit www.joystartshere.com to learn more about each of these options.

## Chris and Jen Thoughts:

*During this exercise Jen and I were able to highlight what helped us grow joy during this past month. We both found that our joy levels have increased and we have been more relational. This means we are more patient, more present and more engaged with each other and our two sons. In such a hard and busy season of life we are grateful for the change. The appreciation step was also encouraging for us. We have decided to go through this handbook again because it has helped us that much. The results are worth the effort and I hope you feel this way as well. May God richly bless your life and family with an increase in joy with Him and each other. Thank you for taking part in this journey with us!*

*For me, Jen, it is hard to believe our thirty days is coming to an end! Thank you for joining us on this journey. We have been delighted to see how much our joy levels have grown and how much better we have been able to handle the overwhelm of this season of life. We are eager to find more creative ways to implement joy on a daily basis. We plan to go through the guide again because we had so much fun! We hope you also had a meaningful month and have decided to continue to make joy a regular part of your life!*

## Additional Resources:

- *Joy Starts Here* at www.joystartshere.com
- *THRIVE 52-week Skill Guides* at www.thrivetoday.org
- *Jesus In Mind* Talks, Volume 28 and 29 at www.joystartshere.com
- *THRIVE Training* at www.thrivetoday.org
    - *Joy Rekindled* Marriage Retreats

## *DAY 30 NOTES - THOUGHTS - OBSERVATIONS:*

# Appendix A
# Immanuel Healing Overview by Dr. Jim Wilder

Developed by E. James Wilder and Chris Coursey for THRIVE Training and Ed Khouri for Connexus for a thriving community life groups © 2009.
Special thanks to Dr. Karl and Charlotte Lehman for Immanuel Interventions and Relational Circuits Test.
Visit www.joystartshere.com for more Share Immanuel resources.

One characteristic of traumatic memories is that they do not include the awareness of the active and relational presence of the true living Jesus with us. The steps involved in bringing the presence of Jesus to our awareness also serve to resolve the traumatic nature of memories.

While we are aware from scriptural promises that Jesus is always with us (Mt. 28:20), when we are upset, overwhelmed or distracted much of our lives go by without an active awareness of God with us - Immanuel. The *Immanuel Approach* has been developed and described by Dr. Karl and Charlotte Lehman, and more information about it can be found on their websites www.kclehman.com, www.outsmartingyourself.org and immanuelapproach.com. We are grateful for their help in articulating and teaching these steps.

Trauma - the incomplete or improper processing of experience into memory - can go wrong at five different levels. While this skill guide is not the place to explain those five levels, it is the place to say that awareness of the active presence of Jesus in our memory does resolve trauma at all five levels. While resolving trauma does not end the story or all suffering, it does allow us to go forward with life and acting responsibly like ourselves.

Our experiences with Jesus are attached to memories just as traumatic events are. To help our minds deal with the times when we are not aware of His presence we begin by remembering the times when we were aware of His presence. Asking Jesus to guide us to a specific memory that will help us connect actively with Him often takes us to a memory we might not have thought about, one with some special characteristic needed for our healing this time.

The Immanuel Process is based on the belief that God is always present with us and always has been. Most of our memories of our life are incomplete because we lack the awareness of God's presence, and without this awareness our interpretations of our life are always distorted, bringing pain and robbing our peace.

The Immanuel Process is based on the belief that God is always able to direct and influence our lives, but we are not always aware of God's presence; often when we do perceive God's presence, we do not recognize it is God.

The Immanuel Process is based on the belief that the accumulation of life experiences and memories in which we are not aware of God's presence makes it more difficult for us to be aware of God and interact with God. The opposite is also true; as we correct our previous memory omissions we are better able to perceive God's presence and recognize when it is God speaking to us.

The Immanuel Process is based on the belief that we will perceive God's presence (and interact with God best) in the areas (memories for the central nervous system) where we have spent the most time with God. These memories reflect the moments when we have had the best relationship with God in the past. We will also have the most pain and confusion in those areas where we have not spent time in relationship with God in the past. Consequently, we should start our times of exploration and healing by returning to the times and memories where we know God best. From these good memories we can better explore those memories where we do not perceive God's presence.

The moments of memory in which we have had a close relationship with God are most open to perceiving God's active presence again in the present. There are several advantages to starting our exploration of the painful and confusing times (where we are not aware of God) by first engaging with God in the places we have known God the best.

1. This is the path with least confusion, distortion and resistance.
2. This is the path that requires us to spend the least amount of time in our pain because we do not begin our search for God's presence while we are sitting on our pain. Instead, we explore our pain while sitting comfortably close to God.

3. Since we begin with an awareness of God that allows us to interact, we can:
    a. Obtain guidance from the start.
    b. Be immediately aware of the point in our memories where we lose the connection with God.
    c. Have a secure point where we can quickly return for comfort and guidance.
    d. Pause an incomplete process in a place of comfort when we are out of time rather than leave someone in his or her pain and confusion.
    e. Complete the healing process in a much shorter time.

We will call these places of close connection with God our "5-bar moments," after the way that cellular phones register a strong signal. Another image would be sitting next to God in a comfortable seat where we can experience God's responses to us. In this position we can pass hours of joy and peace or explore our painful times. The alternative is to sit on the painful sword of our past experiences that lack the awareness of God and try to explore our lives while sitting in pain. Experience has shown that this will work, but it will take about four to six times longer than if we sit in the 5-bar moment memory chair. You will still feel your pain for a moment, but you will not need to stay in it alone.

As mature followers of God, we lead others to the light and help them find the best connection with God. The Immanuel Process finds the best seat is the memories of the times we could hear, fellowship and interact with God. This is the seat we offer those who come for counseling. While there are no places with perfect hearing of God, continued interaction will help us with our distortions and errors.

Not everyone has a 5-bar memory with God. Many people and most Christians only have a sort of "historical sense" of God's presence rather than an interactive sense of God. They have no memories that allow them to return to a secure interaction with God. They cannot be led to the 5-bar location for a good seat. However, there is a second seat available that lets them also explore their memories without sitting on the sword of their pain. This comfortable seat is produced by appreciation of God's gifts and help in the past even when we could not tell directly that God was there. Appreciation of these historical gifts from God allows us to hear more clearly, but with an added difficulty.

This second seat called "appreciation" is close to God, but there is a curtain in our minds between God and us. God still speaks, gives us thoughts, brings things to light, but we cannot tell from this seat if it is God or our own mind that is active. By sitting on the appreciation chair God can guide us to remove the curtain. We will almost always need someone with us who can help us know if we are listening to God or our own minds when we sit in the appreciation chair.

Some people can find the 5-bar chair or the appreciation chair very quickly and stay there easily without falling off the chair and back onto their pain. However, when people fall back into their pain, almost everyone forgets to get back in their chair. Perhaps the most active part of ministering to others is helping people find and stay in their chairs.

There are many who are not able to experience any appreciation memories with God. They cannot find their way to even the second chair with the curtain between them and God.  There are many causes, but those who are ready for healing must desire to interact with God if they are able. They do not need to actually believe in God ahead of time or even like God. For some, the interaction will be more like shouting anger at God, but it is interaction that they want, even if it comes from pain. We cannot even be sure if people desire interaction with God until we find out if their brain's relational circuits are running. When the brain's relational circuits are not working well we neither desire nor perceive our relational resources – including God. This is the nervous system equivalent to trying to see with your eyes closed. Until we open our eyes, we have no chance of seeing (a 5-bar moment) or feeling appreciations for historical relationship moments with God. For this reason, guiding people to desire interaction with God and helping them find a comfortable seat to explore their pain always starts with insuring that people have their relational circuits running. We must also be alert to see if along the way people fall off their chairs or turn off their relational circuits. These are the tasks for the helpers who minister to others.

The Immanuel Process is based on the belief that, while God can and will always speak to us and direct our lives, we cannot perceive God's relationship or even remember God's goodness in a way that feels true or significant as long as our physical relational circuits are off or impaired. Helping people restore their relational circuit functions is often accomplished in several steps.

1. Reduce their fear. "Fear not" is often the first thing God says. We call this step *Shalom My Body.*
2. Validate their distress so they can move beyond broadcasting the distress calls. We call this step *Shalom My Soul.*
3. Comfort their sense of being forsaken by God and others. We call this step *Shalom My Heart.*
4. Respond with appreciation when God and others have lessened our fear, shared our pain, validated and comforted our grief so we are back in a world of relationship possibilities.
5. We can now sit down in the appreciation seat even if there is a curtain in our minds between God and us.

While all the preparations for a wedding may take months of hard work, this preparation should never be confused with the real event. In every Immanuel Process, the moment to take out the cameras and start recording happens when someone becomes aware of the presence of God in a moment where this reality has been missing. To remember pictures we use a camera. To remember events we use a story. The story we want to tell is what happened when our past memories were completed with the active presence of God. It is the telling others about what changed when we were able to perceive the presence of God that helps us remember this 5-bar moment. Telling the story of what changed when we perceived God's presence also changes the way that we see the future. Much of memory is about the past and quickly forgotten when we face a new situation. When we tell the stories of our Immanuel Moments we change the way our minds see the future. It helps us look for God again the next time a similar problem arises. We do not get the same benefit from telling the story of what our life was like BEFORE we experienced the Immanuel moment. That story depresses others and us much like hearing about all the problems preparing for a wedding. The Immanuel Process is based on the belief that we remember best and change the way we think about the future when we tell the story of what changed after we became aware of Immanuel.

## A brief history of the Immanuel Process

Dr. Karl and Charlotte Lehman coined the term "Immanuel Intervention" to describe what happened when their trauma counseling changed its focus from the trauma memory itself to focus on removing blockages that kept people from experiencing the relational presence of Jesus. It has long been observed by people in prayer ministry that traumatic events share a common absence of the active presence of Jesus, and traumas resolve when people experience the active presence of Jesus in the feelings and perceptions created by their incompletely processing the traumatic events. The Lehmans applied two aspects of the Life Model and THRIVE training when they concluded that: 1) our attachment to Jesus is rooted in our attachment memories with Him just as our trauma feelings are rooted in our trauma memories. 2) our brain's relational circuits must be properly functioning for us to perceive the relational presence of Jesus in either our memories or present experience.

These two applications of existing knowledge allowed the Lehmans to focus and refine the steps for healing prayer in their own practice and by the Life Model teachers at Shepherd's House. The Lehman's developed a short "Relational Circuits Test" and the basic steps for restoring the relational circuits. A modified version of the Lehman's test is used in this skill guide. They have prepared extensive and sophisticated teaching materials and proofs for how the Immanuel Intervention works spiritually, practically and neurologically.

## Applications and Resources

Karl Lehman M.D. and Charlotte Lehman (www.kclehman.com, www.outsmartingyourself.org and www.immanuelapproach.com) provide a wealth of training resources from well-documented articles, to teaching series on DVD, to examples of live ministry sessions.

Life Model trainers from THRIVE and Connexus for a thriving community have worked actively with the Lehmans to develop Immanuel training methods for groups. A frequent and liberal exchange of materials and ideas about the Immanuel Intervention, process and lifestyle is now finding its way back to the church.

THRIVE Training (www.thrivetoday.org) considers learning to experience the interactive presence of God as a trainable brain skill. In THRIVE training the Immanuel life style is called "Heartsight," and it is Skill 13 of the 19 essential relational-brain-skills. Teaching people the Immanuel Process is now a standard part of the THRIVE skill training program. THRIVE training should be a strong consideration for leaders who want to develop mature communities and train others.

Connexus for a thriving community (www.joystartshere.com) brings three distinctive elements to churches willing to deal with addictions and trauma. Transforming lives requires multigenerational community, training in relational brain skills and the interactive presence of Jesus in every step. The Immanuel Process is central to teaching the church and people in recovery how to remove whatever blocks us from perceiving God's presence.

Always check your relational circuits when working through this process.

# Appendix B
# Nineteen Gentle Protector Skills

**Skill One: Share Joy.** Mutual amplification of joy through nonverbal facial expressions and voice tone that conveys "We are glad to be together." This capacity allows us to bond and grow strong brains as well.

**Technical description:** Right-hemisphere-to-right-hemisphere communication of our most desired positive emotional state.

**Skill Two: Soothe Myself, Simple Quiet.** Quieting (shalom) after both joyful and upsetting emotions is the strongest predictor of life-long mental health. Lowering my own energy level so I can rest as I need to and on my own makes me feel stable. This self-soothing capacity is the strongest predictor of good mental health for the lifetime.

**Technical description:** Release-on-demand of serotonin by the vegetative branch of parasympathetic nervous system to quiet both positive and distressing emotional states.

**Skill Three: Form Bonds for Two, Synchronize Attachments.** We can share a mutual state of mind that brings us closer and lets us move independently as well. We are both satisfied. The essence of a secure bond is the ability to synchronize our attachment centers so that we can move closer or farther apart at moments that satisfy us both. Synchronized attachment centers provide the basis for smooth transfer of brain skills and learned characteristics.

**Technical description:** Two-way bonds involve simultaneous activation of the attachment centers (*Control Center Level 1*) between two people. This activation helps create a state of mutual mind at the cingulate cortex level (*Control Center Level 3*) that can only be maintained by direct facial contact with one other person at a time.

**Skill Four: Create Appreciation.** High levels of the emotional state of appreciation closely match the healthy balanced state of the brain and nervous system. Creating a strong feeling of appreciation in yourself or others relieves unpleasant states and stress. Appreciation is very similar to the let down reflex that produces milk flow when nursing and the warm contented feeling that follows for mother and child.

**Skill Five: Form Family Bonds, Bonds for Three.** Family bonds allow us to feel joy when people we love have a good relationship with each other. We experience what they feel and understand how they see our relationships through our three-way bonds. Joy bonds between two adults form a couple style bond, so community joy building requires bonds for three or more.

**Technical description:** The prefrontal cortex (*Control Center Level 4*) contains our capacity to maintain three points of view simultaneously.

**Skill Six: Identify Heart Values From Suffering, The Main Pain and Characteristic of Hearts.** Caring deeply can mean hurting deeply. Everyone has issues that particularly hurt or bother him or her and always have been the way he/she is likely to get hurt. Looking at these lifelong issues helps identify the core values for each person's unique identity. We hurt more the more deeply we care. Because of how much pain our deepest values have caused, most people see these characteristics as liabilities not treasures.

**Skill Seven: Tell Synchronized Stories, Four-plus Storytelling.** When our brain is well trained, our capacity is high and we are not triggered by the past; therefore, our whole brain works together. A simple test as well as a means to train the brain is telling stories in a way that requires all the brain to work together.

**Technical description:** The four levels of the right-hemispheric control center work together and allow the bonus (+) of having our words in the left hemisphere match our experience. When emotional and spiritual blockage is resolved our whole brain works in a synchronized way. By selecting stories we can test and train our brains to handle specific aspects of life and relationships.

**Skill Eight: Identify Maturity Levels.** We need to know our ideal maturity level so we know if our development is impaired. Knowing our general (baseline) maturity level tells us what the next developmental tasks will be. Knowing our immediate maturity level from moment to moment lets us know if we have been triggered into reactivity by something that just happened or have encountered a "hole" in our development that needs remedial attention. Watching when our maturity level is slipping also tells us when emotional capacity has been drained in us or others.

**Skill Nine: Take A Breather, Timing When To Disengage.** Sustained closeness and trust requires us to stop and rest before people become overwhelmed when they are tired. These short pauses to quiet and re-charge take only seconds. Those who read the nonverbal cues and let others rest are rewarded with trust and love.

**Technical description:** All the brain-developing and relationship-building moments that create understanding and produce mutual-mind states require paired minds to stop a moment (pause) when the first of the two gets tired, nears overwhelm or is too intensely aroused.

**Skill Ten: Tell Nonverbal Stories.** When we want to strengthen relationships, resolve conflicts or bridge generations or cultures we get much farther with the nonverbal parts of our stories than with words.

**Technical description:** This workout for the nonverbal control center in the right hemisphere develops all the timing and expressive skills used to develop good emotional and relational capacity.

**Skill Eleven: Return To Joy from the Big Six Feelings.** Although we live most of our lives in joy and peace, we need to learn how to stay in relationship and quiet our distress when things go wrong. When we take good care of our relationships even when we are upset the upset does not last long or drive people away. We quickly resolve our "not glad to be together" moments.

**Technical description:** The brain is wired to feel six unpleasant emotions. Fear, anger, sadness, disgust, shame and hopeless despair are each signals of something specific going wrong. We need to learn how to quiet each of these different circuits separately while maintaining our relationships. Training under these six emotional conditions covers the full range of our emotional distress.

**Skill Twelve: Act Like Myself in the Big Six Feelings.** Part of maintaining our relationships when we are upset is learning to act like the same person we were when we had joy to be together. A lack of training or bad examples causes us to damage or withdraw from the relationships we value when we get angry, afraid, sad, disgusted, ashamed or hopeless.

**Skill Thirteen: See What God Sees, Heartsight.** Hope and direction come from seeing situations, ourselves and others the way they were meant to be instead of only seeing what went wrong. This spiritual vision guides our training and restoration. Even forgiveness flows from seeing people's purpose as more important than their malfunctions and makes us a restorative community instead of an accusing one. Through our hearts we see the spiritual vision God sees.

**Skill Fourteen: Stop the Sark.** False "Godsight" may seem true to us at the moment, but leads to blame, accusation, condemnation, gossip, resentment, legalism, self-justification and self-righteousness. This Greek word (also rendered sarx) refers to seeing life from our personal view of who people are and how things should be. This conviction that I know or can determine the right thing to do or be is the opposite of Heartsight in skill thirteen. For the sark, people become what they have done (the sum of their mistakes) or what we want them to become for us.

**Skill Fifteen: Quiet Interactively.** Facial cues, particularly of fear, help us to know when we are pushing others too hard. Sometimes we need and want to maintain a high-energy state without "going over the top," like knowing when to stop tickling so it stays fun. Fast recognition and response to facial cues means optimum interactions and energy.

**Technical description:** Using the ventromedial cortex that is part of Level 4 together with the intelligent branch of the parasympathetic nervous system allows us to control the upper end of arousal states. Instead of taking us all the way to quiet/peace this type of quieting allows us to operate at high levels of energy and quiet just enough to avoid going into overwhelm. This system controls aggressive, sexual and predatory urges so we can avoid harmful behaviors.

**Skill Sixteen: Recognize High and Low Energy Response, Sympathetic and Parasympathetic.** Many characteristic responses to emotions and relationships are strongly shaped by our tendency toward high or low energy reactions. Recognizing who tends to respond with high energy (adrenalin based emotions) and who would rather withdraw helps us match minds with others and bring a more helpful variety to our own response tendencies.

**Skill Seventeen: Identify Attachment Styles.** How well we synchronize our attachments (Skill 3) early in life leaves the most enduring pattern in our personality. These patterns change the way we experience reality. At one end we may give almost no importance to our feelings or relationships and at the other we may feel hurt almost constantly and think of nothing but feelings and people. We may also become afraid of the very people we need. All these factors distort our reality but feel real to us at the time. Knowing how to spot these distortions helps us compensate.

**Skill Eighteen: Intervene Where The Brain is Stuck, Five Distinctive Levels of Brain Disharmony and Pain.** By recognizing the characteristic pain at each of the brain's five levels we can pinpoint the trouble and find a solution if someone gets stuck. The type of pain gives us a good idea of the kind of solution we will need when someone is not "keeping it together," is "falling apart," or is "stuck" as we commonly call these losses of synchronization.

**Technical description:** There are five levels in the brain when we count the four in the right hemisphere control center and add the left hemisphere as the fifth. By knowing the characteristics of each we know when one level got stuck and what kind of interventions will help. For instance, explanations help Level 5 but will not stop a Level 2 terror like the fear of heights.

**Skill Nineteen: Recover from Complex Emotions, Handle Combinations of the Big Six Emotions.** Once we can return to joy and act like ourselves with the six big negative feelings taken one at a time, we can begin to learn how to return to joy and act like ourselves when the six are combined in various combinations. Shame and anger combine to form humiliation. Fear and hopelessness (with almost any other feeling as well) form dread. These combination feelings can be very draining and difficult to quiet.

64366335R00120

Made in the USA
Lexington, KY
06 June 2017